# HIKING THE PACIFIC CREST TRAIL

## PCT – three-part guidebook and map books for thru and section hikers

by David Jordan

JUNIPER HOUSE, MURLEY MOSS,
OXENHOLME ROAD, KENDAL, CUMBRIA LA9 7RL
www.cicerone.co.uk

First edition 2025
ISBN: 978 1 78631 212 9

Printed in China on responsibly sourced paper on behalf of Latitude Press Ltd.
A catalogue record for this book is available from the British Library.
All photographs are by the author unless otherwise stated.

Route mapping by Lovell Johns www.lovelljohns.com
Contains OpenStreetMap.org data © OpenStreetMap contributors, CC-BY-SA.
NASA relief data courtesy of ESRI

## Updates to this guide

While every effort is made by our authors to ensure the accuracy of guidebooks as they go to print, changes can occur during the lifetime of an edition. Any updates that we know of for this guide will be on the Cicerone website (www.cicerone.co.uk/1212/updates), so please check before planning your trip. We also advise that you check information about such things as transport, accommodation and shops locally. Even rights of way can be altered over time. We are always grateful for information about any discrepancies between a guidebook and the facts on the ground, sent by email to updates@cicerone.co.uk.

**Register your book:** To sign up to receive free updates, special offers and GPX files where available, create a Cicerone account and register your purchase via the 'My Account' tab at www.cicerone.co.uk.

*Front cover:* The PCT passes through mountain hemlock trees below Mount Jefferson 10,502ft (3201m)

# CONTENTS

## Warning

The Pacific Crest Trail is designed as a summer trail to be hiked when it is free of snow and the creeks are relatively low. You should be aware that navigation could be difficult and the trail could be dangerous when there is snow in the mountains or when the creeks are running high because of snowmelt. The maps in this guide will not be adequate for navigation when snow covers the trail. If you hike the PCT you will be going into high mountains, wilderness areas and deserts. You might be faced with severe storms, fording unbridged creeks, wildfires, burned areas and hiking through long waterless sections in high temperatures. Mountains and wilderness trekking can be dangerous, carrying the risk of personal injury or death.

## Note on mapping

The route maps in this guide are derived from publicly available data, databases and crowd-sourced data. As such they have not been through the detailed checking procedures that would generally be applied to a published map from an official mapping agency. However, we have reviewed them closely in the light of local knowledge as part of the preparation of this guide.

# Mountain safety

Every mountain walk has its dangers, and those described in this guidebook are no exception. All who walk or climb in the mountains should recognise this and take responsibility for themselves and their companions along the way. The author and publisher have made every effort to ensure that the information contained in this guide was correct when it went to press, but, except for any liability that cannot be excluded by law, they cannot accept responsibility for any loss, injury or inconvenience sustained by any person using this book.

**International distress signal** *(emergency only)*
Six blasts on a whistle (and flashes with a torch after dark) spaced evenly for one minute, followed by a minute's pause. Repeat until an answer is received. The response is three signals per minute followed by a minute's pause.

**Helicopter rescue**
The following signals are used to communicate with a helicopter:

Help needed: raise both arms above head to form a 'Y'

Help not needed: raise one arm above head, extend other arm downward

**Emergency telephone numbers**
In the US the Nationwide Emergency Number is 911

Be prepared to confirm:

1. The location of the emergency
2. The phone number you are calling from
3. The type of the emergency
4. The detail of the emergency

The operator will then transfer you to the appropriate response team.

**Weather reports**
*National Weather Service:* www.weather.gov
*Mountain Weather:* www.mountain-forecast.com

**Mountain rescue can be very expensive – be adequately insured.**

Whitewater River Canyon with San Gorgonio Mountain beyond (Stage 9)

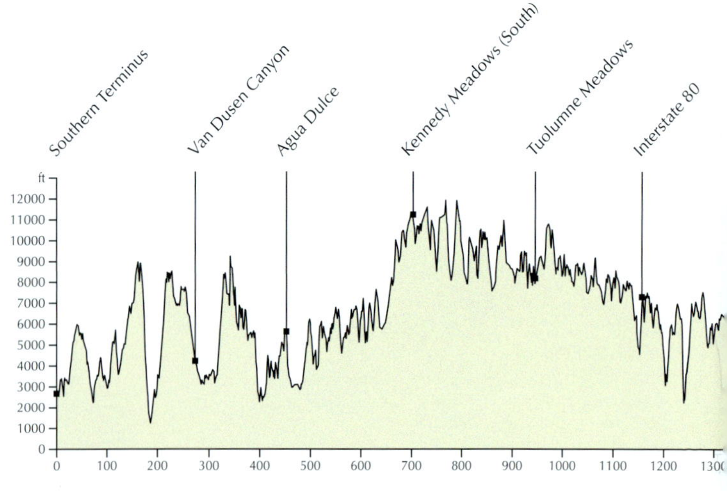

*A stunning rest spot at the head of Rae Lakes (Stage 31)*

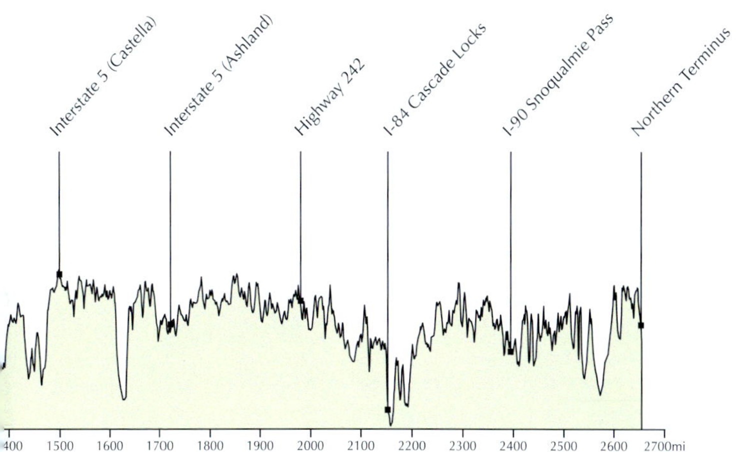

# ROUTE SUMMARY TABLE

| No. | Stage | Distance (miles) | Total ascent (feet) | Total descent (feet) | Duration (hr:min) |
|---|---|---|---|---|---|
| **Section 1** | | | | | |
| 1 | Southern Terminus – Lake Morena | 20.0 | 2451 | 2260 | 9:00 |
| 2 | Lake Morena – Mount Laguna | 22.6 | 3865 | 971 | 10:30 |
| 3 | Mount Laguna – Scissors Crossing | 34.7 | 2034 | 5692 | 14:15 |
| 4 | Scissors Crossing – Warner Springs | 32.2 | 3635 | 2831 | 13:30 |
| 5 | Warner Springs – Chihuahua Valley Rd | 17.8 | 2927 | 942 | 8:00 |
| 6 | Chihuahua Valley Rd – Hwy 74 | 24.6 | 3110 | 3228 | 11:10 |
| 7 | Hwy 74 – Saddle Junction | 27.5 | 6791 | 3586 | 14:15 |
| 8 | Saddle Junction – San Gorgonio Pass | 30.1 | 2431 | 9206 | 15:50 |
| 9 | San Gorgonio Pass – Onyx Summit | 42.6 | 10,853 | 3652 | 20:00 |
| 10 | Onyx Summit – Van Dusen Canyon | 23.0 | 1742 | 3018 | 10:30 |
| **Totals** | | **275.1** | **39,839** | **35,386** | **126:30** |
| **Section 2** | | | | | |
| 11 | Van Dusen Canyon – Hwy 173 | 39.2 | 3432 | 7503 | 14:30 |
| 12 | Hwy 173 – Hwy 138 | 14.8 | 1266 | 974 | 6:00 |
| 13 | Hwy 138 – Cajon Pass | 12.9 | 1302 | 1690 | 5:40 |
| 14 | Cajon Pass – Hwy 2 Inspiration Point | 27.4 | 6263 | 1916 | 14:15 |
| 15 | Hwy 2 Inspiration Point – Hwy 2 Islip Saddle | 16.6 | 3714 | 4413 | 8:40 |
| 16 | Hwy 2 Islip Saddle – Mill Crk Summit | 32.6 | 5525 | 7320 | 14:40 |
| 17 | Mill Crk Summit – North Fork Ranger Station | 17.5 | 2867 | 3609 | 7:30 |
| 18 | North Fork Ranger Station – Agua Dulce | 18.4 | 1965 | 3612 | 8:00 |
| **Totals** | | **179.4** | **26,334** | **31,037** | **79:15** |

| No. | Stage | Distance (miles) | Total ascent (feet) | Total descent (feet) | Duration (hr:min) |
|---|---|---|---|---|---|
| **Section 3** | | | | | |
| 19 | Agua Dulce – Lake Hughes Rd | 31.2 | 5092 | 4554 | 14:30 |
| 20 | Lake Hughes Rd – Hwy 138 | 31.9 | 4619 | 4639 | 14:30 |
| 21 | Hwy 138 – Cottonwood Crk | 17.3 | 548 | 495 | 6:35 |
| 22 | Cottonwood Crk – Tehachapi Pass | 31.5 | 4849 | 4137 | 14:50 |
| 23 | Tehachapi Pass – Piute Mountain Rd | 42.9 | 7444 | 5036 | 19:20 |
| 24 | Piute Mountain Rd – Bird Spring Pass | 22.7 | 2992 | 3862 | 9:40 |
| 25 | Bird Spring Pass – Walker Pass | 21.2 | 3222 | 3314 | 9:10 |
| 26 | Walker Pass – Chimney Creek CG | 28.9 | 5115 | 4826 | 13:30 |
| 27 | Chimney Creek CG – Kennedy Meadows | 21.3 | 3153 | 2703 | 9:40 |
| **Totals** | | **248.9** | **37,034** | **33,566** | **111:45** |
| **Section 4** | | | | | |
| 28 | Kennedy Meadows – Trail Pass | 43.1 | 7972 | 3494 | 21:45 |
| 29 | Trail Pass – Crabtree Meadow | 21 | 2756 | 2887 | 9:30 |
| 30 | Crabtree Meadow – Kearsarge Pass Trail | 22.6 | 5394 | 5016 | 12:50 |
| 31 | Kearsarge Pass Trail – Taboose Pass Trail | 21.3 | 4780 | 4728 | 13:15 |
| 32 | Taboose Pass Trail – Bishop Pass Trail | 20.8 | 2759 | 4790 | 10:00 |
| 33 | Bishop Pass Trail – Piute Pass Trail | 24.9 | 3379 | 4052 | 12:20 |
| 34 | Piute Pass Trail – Bear Ridge Trail | 18.6 | 4049 | 2231 | 10:10 |
| 35 | Bear Ridge Trail – Red's Meadow | 32.1 | 5604 | 7792 | 14:45 |
| 36 | Red's Meadow – Tuolumne Meadows | 35.9 | 4990 | 4094 | 16:25 |
| **Totals** | | **240.3** | **41,683** | **39,084** | **121:00** |
| **Section 5** | | | | | |
| 37 | Tuolumne Meadows – Bear Valley Trail | 37.2 | 6775 | 7372 | 19:00 |
| 38 | Bear Valley Trail – Sonora Pass | 37.2 | 6348 | 4689 | 18:50 |
| 39 | Sonora Pass – Ebbetts Pass | 31.5 | 5384 | 6335 | 14:45 |
| 40 | Ebbetts Pass – Carson Pass | 28.3 | 4285 | 4432 | 12:10 |

| No. | Stage | Distance (miles) | Total ascent (feet) | Total descent (feet) | Duration (hr:min) |
|---|---|---|---|---|---|
| 41 | Carson Pass – Echo Lake | 15.5 | 2018 | 3150 | 6:45 |
| 42 | Echo Lake – Barker Pass | 32.6 | 4908 | 4485 | 14:50 |
| 43 | Barker Pass – Interstate 80 | 32.2 | 5236 | 5659 | 14:50 |
| **Totals** | | **214.5** | **34,954** | **36,122** | **101:10** |
| **Section 6** | | | | | |
| 44 | Interstate 80 – Hwy 49 Sierra City | 38.4 | 4547 | 7205 | 16:20 |
| 45 | Hwy 49 Sierra City – Quincy LaPorte Rd | 39.4 | 7664 | 5712 | 18:35 |
| 46 | Quincy LaPorte Road – Big Creek Rd | 28.7 | 5023 | 5984 | 12:40 |
| 47 | Big Creek Rd – Hwy 70 Belden | 23.4 | 2300 | 5627 | 9:45 |
| 48 | Hwy 70 Belden – Humboldt Summit | 24.7 | 6811 | 2356 | 13:45 |
| 49 | Humboldt Summit – Hwy 36 nr Chester | 19.5 | 2218 | 3819 | 8:20 |
| 50 | Hwy 36 nr Chester – Hat Creek Resort | 42.1 | 4455 | 4961 | 18:15 |
| 51 | Hat Creek Resort – Road 22 | 20.1 | 1112 | 1066 | 8:00 |
| 52 | Road 22 – Burney Falls | 25.5 | 669 | 2323 | 9:50 |
| 53 | Burney Falls – Bartle Gap | 27 | 4678 | 2510 | 13:00 |
| 54 | Bartle Gap – McCloud River | 25 | 2612 | 5302 | 10:20 |
| 55 | McCloud River – I-5 (Castella) | 30.2 | 5039 | 5335 | 13:35 |
| **Totals** | | **344** | **47,128** | **52,200** | **152:25** |
| **Section 7** | | | | | |
| 56 | I-5 (Castella) – Parks Creek Rd | 38.5 | 7165 | 2451 | 19:00 |
| 57 | Parks Creek Rd – Hwy 3 | 20.5 | 886 | 2372 | 8:00 |
| 58 | Hwy 3 – Carter Meadows Summit | 19.8 | 3077 | 2283 | 9:10 |
| 59 | Carter Meadows Summit – Etna Summit | 19.7 | 3789 | 4019 | 9:50 |
| 60 | Etna Summit – Paradise Lake | 29.1 | 5387 | 5223 | 13:55 |
| 61 | Paradise Lake – Seiad Valley | 27.1 | 1886 | 6706 | 10:00 |
| 62 | Seiad Valley – Cook and Green Pass | 14.8 | 5157 | 1762 | 9:35 |
| 63 | Cook and Green Pass – Wrangle Gap | 27.6 | 4954 | 3228 | 13:00 |

| No. | Stage | Distance (miles) | Total ascent (feet) | Total descent (feet) | Duration (hr:min) |
|---|---|---|---|---|---|
| 64 | Wrangle Gap – I-5 (Ashland) | 20.4 | 1831 | 4062 | 8:30 |
| **Totals** | | **217.5** | **34,132** | **32,106** | **101:00** |
| **Section 8** | | | | | |
| 65 | I-5 (Ashland) – Hyatt Lake | 23.9 | 3776 | 2835 | 10:00 |
| 66 | Hyatt Lake – Dead Indian Memorial Rd | 18.9 | 2812 | 2536 | 8:10 |
| 67 | Dead Indian Memorial Rd – Red Lake Trail | 25.2 | 2667 | 2047 | 10:15 |
| 68 | Red Lake Trail – Sevenmile Trail | 17.4 | 1877 | 2172 | 7:25 |
| 69 | Sevenmile Trail – Hwy 62 | 16.8 | 1969 | 1604 | 7:40 |
| 70 | Hwy 62 – Hwy 138 | 26.9 | 1850 | 2083 | 10:00 |
| 71 | Hwy 138 – Windigo Pass | 30.4 | 3330 | 3445 | 12:30 |
| 72 | Windigo Pass – Hwy 58 Williamette Pass | 29.7 | 3294 | 4012 | 12:30 |
| 73 | Hwy 58 Williamette Pass – Irish Lake | 22.7 | 2753 | 2277 | 9:30 |
| 74 | Irish Lake – Horse Lake Trail (Elk Lake) | 23.2 | 1486 | 1755 | 8:50 |
| 75 | Horse Lake Trail (Elk Lake) – Hwy 242 McKenzie Pass | 29.9 | 3894 | 3927 | 12:55 |
| **Totals** | | **265** | **29,708** | **28,693** | **109:45** |
| **Section 9** | | | | | |
| 76 | Hwy 242 McKenzie Pass – Santiam Pass | 17.1 | 1739 | 2201 | 7:10 |
| 77 | Santiam Pass – Milk Crk | 27.6 | 3737 | 4134 | 12:25 |
| 78 | Milk Crk – Breitenbush Lake | 12.2 | 2697 | 1542 | 6:30 |
| 79 | Breitenbush Lake – Road 42 | 34.4 | 2851 | 4885 | 14:05 |
| 80 | Road 42 – Barlow Pass | 18.1 | 2001 | 1293 | 7:25 |
| 81 | Barlow Pass – Lolo Pass | 22.7 | 4439 | 5207 | 11:15 |
| 82 | Lolo Pass – Wahtum Lake | 16.4 | 2244 | 1768 | 6:40 |
| 83 | Wahtum Lake – I-84 Cascade Locks | 16.1 | 2005 | 5620 | 7:00 |
| **Totals** | | **164.6** | **21,713** | **26,650** | **72:30** |

| No. | Stage | Distance (miles) | Total ascent (feet) | Total descent (feet) | Duration (hr:min) |
|---|---|---|---|---|---|
| **Section 10** | | | | | |
| 84 | I-84 Cascade Locks – Wind River Rd | 33.3 | 6447 | 5571 | 15:55 |
| 85 | Wind River Rd – Road 24 | 34.8 | 6152 | 2999 | 16:00 |
| 86 | Road 24 – Road 23 | 14.1 | 1808 | 2159 | 6:15 |
| 87 | Road 23 – Road 5603 | 22.2 | 3038 | 2198 | 10:20 |
| 88 | Road 5603 – Hwy 12 near White Pass | 43.8 | 6709 | 7116 | 21:15 |
| 89 | Hwy 12 near White Pass – Chinook Pass | 28.6 | 4580 | 3550 | 14:45 |
| 90 | Chinook Pass – Road 784 | 32 | 4327 | 4833 | 13:50 |
| 91 | Road 784 – Stampede Pass | 19.4 | 3383 | 4626 | 8:30 |
| 92 | Stampede Pass – I-90 Snoqualmie Pass | 18.3 | 3268 | 3973 | 8:20 |
| **Totals** | | **246.5** | **39,712** | **37,025** | **115:10** |
| **Section 11** | | | | | |
| 93 | I-90 Snoqualmie Pass – Waptus River | 34.7 | 7549 | 7467 | 18:55 |
| 94 | Waptus River – Stevens Pass | 36.2 | 7474 | 6476 | 19:40 |
| 95 | Stevens Pass – Indian Pass | 34.2 | 7041 | 6148 | 17:00 |
| 96 | Indian Pass – Suiattle River | 42.3 | 8107 | 10696 | 19:50 |
| 97 | Suiattle River – Stehekin River | 31.3 | 5000 | 5850 | 13:20 |
| 98 | Stehekin River – Rainy Pass | 19.3 | 4580 | 1325 | 9:20 |
| 99 | Rainy Pass – Hart's Pass | 30.9 | 5922 | 4577 | 14:50 |
| 100 | Hart's Pass – Northern Terminus | 30.5 | 4485 | 6424 | 14:30 |
| **Totals** | | **259.4** | **50,158** | **48,963** | **127:25** |
| Exit from Northern Terminus to Manning Park | | 8.8 | 1112 | 1457 | 4:00 |

# INTRODUCTION

Bullfrog Lake from Kearsage Pass (Stage 30)

It is difficult to introduce a trail of such variety, but that is in fact the essence of what makes the Pacific Crest Trail what it is. It traverses an enormous distance, approximately 2655 miles, from the southern border of the United States with Mexico, across three states, 48 wilderness areas, 25 national forests and six national parks to reach the northern border with Canada. Few who hike the PCT will remain unchanged by it, whether they hike some of it, all of it stage by stage, or undertake the epic journey of a single end to end 'thru-hike'.

The major regions crossed by the trail include the Sonoran and Mojave deserts, the foothills and mountains of the Sierra Nevada range, and the Cascade Range which showcases a vast variety of volcanic forms as it roams from high passes to deep forests. Crossing streams and creeks, and passing glistening lakes, this is a narrow, rugged corridor through the best of the landscapes that the American west has to offer.

However, most hikers who spend time here find that the real beauty of the trail lies not in the large expanses of landscape and sky (impressive as they are), but rather in the smaller aspects of trail life, away from the demands and stresses of everyday 'normal' life, where relaxed and at ease, we cease to look inward and start to observe the world around us. These are the details that intrigue and inspire when we are immersed in nature and have the time to wonder about the plants and flowers, the insects that shelter under them or feed upon them, the small creatures that scurry about collecting our lunch crumbs, or how the rocks we sit on came to be there.

The experience is not only a natural one, but also a human one. We share the trail with other hikers, who have come from near and far to experience the PCT. That shared experience brings us closer together. The vulnerability we come to understand in a mountain storm, or at a raging creek crossing, is humbling, then the security and reassurance of others overcomes differences of language, culture or views, and we find in the shared experience, the basis of friendship.

*Looking south from Forester Pass (Stage 30)*

Enjoyment of the trail undoubtedly requires finding a balance between the demands of the hiking, the weight of the load, the comfort in camp and the progress that brings the experiences we seek. With modern, lightweight equipment that balance is more achievable than ever, but no hiker wants to carry more than is necessary for the enjoyment of the trail. It is with that in mind that this guide has been created as three volumes, such that only a third of it need ever be carried to benefit from all that it offers.

Hikers should find that having a guide and map, adds context to the landscape around the narrow trail corridor, it enables translation of the land and security if a phone or GPS is lost or fails. A narration of the route is rarely needed, but here and there the trail is vague, or choices could be made, and at these points select information and guidance are valuable. A map is easier to follow on paper and can be consulted repeatedly without a drain on batteries.

The experience that has contributed to the content of this guide is drawn from five thru-hikes of the PCT. Three by the first author of this guide in 2002, 2006 and 2009, then two by this author in 2016 and 2023. It is hoped that through the evolution of this guide, we have achieved a good balance between effective mapping, useful advice/information, and a format that keeps weight to the absolute minimum. I sincerely hope it adds value to your hike/s.

## CAN AN 'ORDINARY' PERSON HIKE THE PCT?

It is astonishing what an ordinary person can do when they put their mind to it. You do not need to be an athlete, or have special skills, you don't even need experience, you will accumulate that as you hike. Walking is what our bodies have evolved to do, it is what we are designed for. If we have a little trouble getting started, and get a bit sore, it is only that we have become too used to being seated. There are so many examples of 'ordinary' people, achieving their goal to hike the PCT.

- In 2000, Dennis thru-hiked following a heart and lung transplant the year before
- In 2004, Mary, a 10-year-old girl, thru-hiked the trail with her parents
- In 2006, a 22-year-old hiker needed a month off trail after being bitten by a brown recluse spider. She still reached Canada in late October that year
- In 2002, Brian, the first author of this guide completed the trail after early retirement due to a serious foot injury
- In 2016, Luke stood at the southern terminus and took his first ever hiking steps before his first ever tent-night. Five months later he completed the trail

What they all had in common was a belief they could do it, and a determination to overcome each problem that arose. If they can do it, so can you.

*Potest quia posse videntur* – 'They can because they think they can'

*The southern terminus and Mexican border (Stage 1)*

## THE PCT ROUTE AND TRAIL

Starting from the Mexican border, at a monument around 50 miles east of San Diego, the Pacific Crest Trail meanders its way north for around 2655 miles, through the combined length of California, Oregon and Washington, all the way to a corresponding monument at the Canadian Border about 100 miles east of Vancouver, British Columbia. As the name suggests, it follows the crest of the mountains, rising and falling with the watershed divide, exploring the panorama that becomes visible, only from the higher ground.

Camping on the shore of West Swan Lake, north of Highway 140 (Stage 67)

In Europe, long-distance trails are invariably pieced together from historic footpaths that date back centuries. By nature, these evolved from the traffic of people from place to place, and so lead, with some inevitability, between and through settlements and communities. In the US, long-distance trails are built with an entirely different philosophy, routed to avoid settlements and places, designed to maximize the wilderness experience. As a wilderness trail that only occasionally touches on civilisation, wilderness camping is a key part of the experience, as is the periodic departure from the trail to resupply with food, and anything else needed.

Designed for the exclusive use of hikers and horse riders, it shares only a handful of miles with other users on paved or dirt roads, and is a largely well-engineered trail, designed at moderate gradients with the regular use of switchbacks on steep ground. However, that does not always mean it is easy to walk. Flood, landslip, constant vegetation

There is little shade on the exposed hills of Owens Peak Wilderness (Stage 25)

re-growth, avalanche damage, tree fall, and wildfire damage all combine to ensure that the work of the trail builders is never over.

This also ensures that, while the overall route is now well established, the actual distance changes by small amounts almost every year because of trail repair and maintenance. Such change may be to circumvent landslips, to minimize excessive erosion or sometimes the result of changes on private land where the PCT is granted permissive access. In addition, new land is occasionally purchased by the PCTA in a bid to make small improvements to the route or to take the trail through a protected corridor rather than across private land. In any given year these small changes in trail alignment can lengthen or reduce the overall trail distance. Consequently, you will notice that sources often differ very slightly on the exact mileage at any given point.

## HISTORY

Unsurprisingly most discourse on hiking the Pacific Crest Trail rightly highlights the wealth of natural beauty, wildlife and landscape features that are there to explore, along with the rare opportunity this presents in the modern world to slow down and reflect, in a philosophical way, on our lives and relationship to the natural world. There is much to explore on the trail too however, of human history: the indigenous American tribes and the pioneers whose own exploration of these western landscapes contributed to the development of America as we know it today, from the westward expansion of the early colonies to the formation of the United States. Traces of both the indigenous people and these early settler journeys west can be found in the names of peaks and passes, in places where memorials are dedicated, and in the small communities that neighbour the trail where the stories and memories live on.

The mountain crest that forms the backbone of the trail was once the primary barrier to westward expansion and settlement. It proved a fierce obstacle for some years and resulted in tales of daring and disaster, such as that which befell the Donner Party in 1846 when they became trapped in heavy winter snows in the Sierra Nevada. After the pioneers came the settlers, and the routes west across the mountains became established. The PCT crosses these west-bound emigration trails, such as the 2170-mile Oregon Trail and the 1600-mile California Trail, on its way north.

It was a surprisingly short space of time from the early crossings of these mountains to settlers starting to look to them for recreation. The first recorded backpacking trip dates from 1913 (between Kennedy Meadows North and Lake Tahoe), although undoubtedly there were earlier such trips that did not leave a written record. The first notion of a crest trail to run through the Cascades and south to join the Sierra of California seems likely to have originated from one Fred W. Cleator, a Forest Service ranger in Oregon in 1918, although a teacher called Catherine Montgomery, from Bellingham, Washington, is also often credited with the idea in 1926. In the 1930s Clinton C. Clarke, a keen outdoorsman, took up the campaign for such a trail, eventually leading the formation of the Pacific Crest Trail System Conference and serving as its president for 25 years. Clarke also published the first guidebook loosely describing the trail's route.

In 1946 Joseph T. Hazard published *Pacific Crest Trails* (Superior Publishing Co.) describing a quite astounding variety of mountain adventures undertaken across the 1920s, 1930s and 1940s, not only down the length of the US Pacific Crest, but from Alaska to Cape Horn. His ambition was enormous, espousing the possibility of a Pan-American trail to rival the developing highway.

*Snow patch on the north side of Forester Pass in Stage 30 (photo: James Humenansky)*

*Vasquez Rocks, south of Agua Dulce has been used as the set of many movies (Stage 18)*

While this did not reach fruition, it certainly played a part in establishing in the minds of the public, the notion of a pan-US Pacific Crest Trail.

In 1968, following the report of a commission into walking trails, the National Trails System Act was passed recognizing the Appalachian and Pacific Crest Trails as the first two National Scenic Trails. However, it was not until 1993, after lengthy challenges with private landowners that the 'Golden Spike Dedication' declared the PCT complete.

*The active glaciers on Mount Adams can be heard moving from the PCT (Stage 87)*

## THE REGIONS

Often described just as 'the desert', the PCT in Southern California is quite varied in landscape, flora and fauna. The route crosses long dry stretches of chaparral interspersed with rolling hills and mountains. Forests are only present at higher, cooler elevations where views are extensive. The crossing of the western corner of the Mojave Desert is hot and quite dry, and the hiker is glad to climb into the Tehachapi Mountains where the rising desert winds accelerate through the pass. Beyond, at Walker Pass, the Sierra Nevada range begins, although the change is gradual until beyond Kennedy Meadows.

From Kennedy Meadows to Donner Pass through Central California, the trail traverses 450 miles of spectacular alpine landscape. Crossing a succession of passes above 11,000ft the route

*Silhouetted Joshua Tree at Walker Pass campground (Stage 25)*

remains above treeline for much of the time. Forester Pass is the trail high-point at 13,153ft, but take a short side-trip and you can top Mount Whitney at 14,421ft, the highest peak in the lower 48 states. For 200 miles north the PCT coincides with the famous John Muir Trail (JMT) through a stunning vista of snow-capped peaks and jewel-like lakes. North of Carson Pass the trail coincides for 50 miles with the western reaches of the Tahoe Rim Trail.

Soon after Donner Pass you enter the southern end of the Cascade Range. The landscape becomes unmistakably volcanic, and the forests thicken on rich, moist soils. The trail passes Mount Lassen and crosses Lassen Volcanic National Park, dipping into Old Station and past Subway Cave before climbing to cross the exposed plateau of Hat Creek Rim. After briefly visiting the spectacular Burney Falls, the PCT trends west into the Trinity Alps, at the start of a grand arc around the west slope of Mount Shasta, eventually crossing into Oregon.

Oregon offers the hiker easier trails with less ascent than elsewhere on the PCT. Here the landscape is dominated by volcanos and lava flows. Most will hike the Crater Lake

*The John Muir Hut atop Muir Pass (Stage 33)*

*Crossing the Bridge of the Gods over the Columbia River requires a head for heights (Stage 84)*

alternate in order not to miss this wonder of the natural world. Beyond, the forests are dotted with turquoise lakes that invite a swim. The trail continues north past the Three Sisters, Three Fingered Jack and Mount Jefferson, before ascending the slopes of Mount Hood to visit the historic Timberline Lodge. The Eagle Creek alternate is another highlight on the descent into Cascade Locks and the famous Bridge of the Gods, at the lowest point of the trail, just 99ft.

Washington's temperate rainforests are lush with moisture, with mosses and lichens dripping from the trees. Camp under Mount Adams and the creak of glaciers will accompany your dreams. Beyond, Old Snowy Mountain marks the start of the airy traverse of Goat Rocks Ridge, where the fortunate may spot the namesake goats themselves. Roads here become scarce, and a sense of remoteness accompanies you through Glacier Peak Wilderness to tiny Stehekin at the head of the great Lake Chelan. The final miles don't disappoint with high ridges and vast views until the final descent to the border.

## THE SECTIONS AND STAGES

In planning terms, the PCT is too long to think about in its entirety, not least as it includes incredibly diverse landscapes and conditions, which affect choices of gear, time of year, when and where to resupply, right down to where to camp and find adequate water. It is necessary to break the trail down into manageable chunks, whether to hike in sections, or as a way of planning the logistics of a thru-hike.

Early guides adopted a lettering system from A to R in California, then starting back at A through to L in Oregon and Washington, with an anomaly bound to confuse; Section R in California and Section A in Oregon were the same section repeated. These 29 sections ranged from 38 to 175 miles and remain in use on many maps and guides.

Brian Johnson, the first author of this guidebook, devised a different approach. One hundred stages broken into eleven sections. This structure hopes to offer the section hiker an easier way to plan and think about smaller hikes, that can easily be 'chunked' together when more time is available for longer outings. At the same time the thru-hiker might appreciate the manageable scale that encourages them to think, typically a day or two ahead in each stage while tent sites and water sources are the priority, yet still relate to a larger structure in which opportunities for rest and resupply become the priority.

*Trail sign marks the California/ Oregon border (Stage 63)*

In this structure, Sections 1–3 take the hiker across the desert, from the Southern Terminus to Kennedy Meadows South, just before the Sierra Nevada mountains. These sections break, first at Van Dusen Canyon where there is good access to Big Bear Lake, and second at Agua Dulce, just off Highway 14 between Santa Clarita and Palmdale. Sections 4 and 5 take the hiker across the Sierra Nevada range, breaking at Tuolumne Meadows and then at Interstate 80 outside of Truckee. Sections 6 and 7 cover Northern California, initially to the first crossing of Interstate 5, not too far from Mount Shasta, then to the second crossing of Interstate 5, close to Ashland. At this point the trail has crossed into Oregon and Sections

8 and 9 take the hiker as far as the Washington border at Cascade Locks, breaking at McKenzie Pass, a short hop from the town of Sisters. Finally, Sections 10 and 11 cross Washington, breaking at Snoqualmie Pass before finally reaching the Northern Terminus at the border with Canada.

*Serendipity: a tree falls across the trail, breaking at the perfect place to allow passage (Stage 26)*

## DAY HIKES, SECTIONS AND THRU-HIKES

All manner of people hike the PCT. Most don't have the luxury of the time or money to contemplate committing up to six months to attempt the whole trail in one go and may have no desire to. Yet that should stop no one from experiencing the trail, whether they only ever walk a few stages, or spend a lifetime piecing them together. The great majority of hikes on the PCT will be undertaken in a single day, using trailheads to access an area, and returning home at the end of the day. This approach has the great advantage of enabling spontaneity, with little needed in the way of planning or permits, nor much in the way of specialist equipment.

Section-hikers are often either those who want to enjoy just their own choice of sections or stages, or those keen to experience the whole trail, but who prefer to do so in manageable chunks that can be fitted in around the many other aspects of their lives. For some, choosing to section-hike

*The descent into Whitewater River Canyon (Stage 9)*

*Ascending snow-clad slopes in Marble Mountain Wilderness (Stage 60)*

an entire trail over many years, can be a great antidote to the stresses of modern life. The structure provided by gradually completing stages can be motivating, giving a sense of purpose and achievement, and provide a chance to regularly reconnect with nature and re-energize.

It could also be argued that a distinct advantage of section-hiking is the chance to experience each stage of trail at the optimum season for the weather and conditions. This may mean early, if you want to catch big mountains with snow-capped peaks and spring flowers, or later if perhaps you want the autumnal color and the least intrusion of mosquitos!

It is certainly the case however, that thru-hikers have an immersive, absorbing experience that truly becomes a way of life for a time, and that is undoubtedly a privilege. Most who have thru-hiked would argue that it changes you and your relationship with the world in a whole host of ways. However, with the scale of a thru-hike comes the ever-present awareness of the limitations of time and the seasons; that pressure to keep moving and cover the miles before the weather window starts to close. It is harder on a thru-hike to carve out the time to go slow, explore off the main route, or just sit and absorb the landscape and wildlife.

## PLANNING A THRU-HIKE

While this section is aimed at those considering a thru-hike, most of it will be as relevant to anyone planning a long section. Either way, the planning stage is probably the most important in determining your success. You don't need to be super-fit, in fact with a little training and preparation most people could undertake a long-distance thru-hike. However, the statistics that are available loosely suggest that in a typical year less than 25%, or one in four people, complete the hike they set out to do.

### Deciding to go

Undoubtedly the decision is the hardest part. For most, a thru-hike means 'parking' normal life for many months, whether that be family commitments, jobs, careers or education, and making the necessary arrangements to be absent for a while. It seems daunting and it's no surprise that many people never get beyond 'thinking about it'. Making it happen requires making a firm decision first. If you wait until you've found answers to all the questions related to how, you'll never go. Taking a leap of faith is empowering.

*South Brown Mountain Shelter, north of Dead Indian Memorial Road (Stage 67)*

*Haze over Chimney Peak Wilderness (Stage 26)*

If it is what you really want, decide, fix a date, then tell someone, in fact tell everyone (it makes it harder to back out), then make a plan.

### Which direction?

An early decision will be whether to go northbound (nobo), southbound (sobo) or to do a little of each by 'flipping' ahead, then returning to a section, perhaps when conditions are better (flip-flop). Most will choose a nobo hike. It is a longer season, easier to get to the start, the initial terrain is easier and there will be more hikers around for company. If conditions are challenging in any given year however, it can be useful to change to a flip-flop approach.

### When to go

The next consideration is when to start. This choice may be quite constrained by permits (see Permits and regulations) however in an average weather year a mid–late April start would allow plenty of time to go slow initially without reaching the Sierra Nevada too early when snow is still deep. In an average year, June 15 is about the right time to enter the Sierra section when the snow melt and creeks become passable. In a drier year you could start earlier, and later in a wet (snowy) year.

Having a plan is critical to success. You won't stick to it, but it gives you a reference point to know what is required to 'make it', and so you

*The trail takes an airy path blasted into the slopes of Huckleberry Mountain (Stage 93)*

know when you've fallen behind and need to catch up, or if you've got ahead you might want to add in a rest day or just slow down a bit and relax more. So, how do I make a plan?

## Making a plan

If you've chosen a direction, and have a target start date, the next thing to do is work out how long it will take. How long depends on your daily mileage and how many rest days you take. At an average of just 15 miles per day, you could complete the trail in 177 days, a little under six months. If your daily average increased to 17.5 miles, you would take about five months. If you're not sure, to find the daily average over any given distance, divide the total distance by the total number of days you plan to take, including any zero (or 'rest') days.

*Average daily mileage = distance / total elapsed days (both hiking and zero days)*

In practice you'll want to start slow and build up gradually to protect yourself from injury. Plus, each rest day will reduce your daily average. So, let's say you want to average 12 miles per day in the first 100 miles. Divide the distance by the miles per day (100 / 12 = 8.3) and you can see it will take 8.3 days to cover the first 100 miles. Repeat this exercise along the trail, gradually increasing your daily average mileage, perhaps to around 23–25 per day by the later stages of North California, and you will soon see how long the whole thing will take you. This is the start of your plan.

To take some of the guess work out of planning, this guide provides a table in Appendix D with an overview of the trail, the key resupply points (there are many others too) the mileage and an indication of how many hours of walking are required between resupply points at a very moderate pace (a little under 2.2 miles per hour). The table then provides a schedule showing approximately how many hours of walking and how many miles you would need to walk each day, to cover the whole trail in 110 days, 120 days 130 days and so on, up to a 180-day schedule. Most hikers will be walking faster than this once they are fit and accustomed to trail life, but it provides a good basis for planning.

### What about budget?

Planning a budget depends on things like how much suitable equipment you already have, and your choices around both equipment and food. If you're starting from scratch, equipment could cost as much as $2000. Food resupply will likely cost upwards of $3000. Then there are town expenses (hotels, restaurants, laundry, postal costs), donations for rides, replacing shoes up to five times and so on! Once you are hiking, time spent in town can sap your budget

*Approaching Tehachapi you pass among hundreds of wind turbines (Stage 22)*

quickly. A zero day will require town accommodation, probably a restaurant meal or two and other expenses. It is not uncommon for thru-hikers to spend in excess of $8000 in total. One way to minimize this cost is the use of 'nearo' (or 'nero') days (hiker slang for 'part-days') instead of whole days in town. Aim to reach a trailhead late in the day, camp nearby and hitch into town in the morning. Do your resupply shopping, get lunch from a supermarket deli or similar and get out of town, ideally with enough time to walk a few miles before camping. It is far more relaxing to spend a day at a lake if you need a rest day. This approach keeps cost to the minimum and affects your average daily mileage less.

### Hiking discipline

Hiking a long trail takes discipline. Know how many hours a day you will need to walk to achieve your target daily distance. Once you have built

*Approaching Rock Pass close to the border (Stage 100)*

*Sandy trail in Domeland Wilderness on the way to Kennedy Meadows (Stage 27)*

up fitness you will probably need to hike between 7 and 10 hours each day to stay on track. If you get up early and get moving quickly you can then afford to break the day with one or more good rests, which helps minimize the chance of blisters and overuse injuries. For example, in the hot desert you could get going as early as possible, get as far as possible then rest across the hottest part of the day, walk for a couple of afternoon hours, stop for dinner then walk again in the cooler evening.

The more training you do, the easier the early days will be. Get your gear together well before your planned start and go for regular walks with a full pack. Pitch your tent and sleep out too, even if that is in the yard or garden.

## THE FIRST WEEK

As many as one in four hikers that start the trail, quit within the first week. With that sobering statistic in mind, it is worth preparing to ensure that is not you. You already have a plan, so are in a better place than many.

- Mental preparation is key. Lower your expectations for the first week. Be aware that there will be a lot of 'noise' among other hikers initially, sharing doubts and anxieties. Expect this and ignore it. Stay off social media groups and avoid speculation. You've done your homework, and you have a plan, you can be quietly confident.
- Know that your body will ache as it adjusts to the weight of your pack, and the routine of daily hiking. This is normal and will not last, each day it will get stronger. Stretch regularly, and air your feet often. Address any soreness immediately and avoid sunburn. Preventing injuries in this first week is your priority. Don't hike more than you planned, even if you feel good, and avoid getting caught up with what others are doing.
- Make small adjustments to your pack and gear. Try alternating the weight between your shoulders and hips. Experiment with tent pitches and packing until you find a rhythm and approach that works for you. Consider whether you are carrying anything that could really be sent home to lighten your pack.
- Develop efficient hiking habits too. Hydrate well each morning before you hike. Rise early and walk in the cooler morning. Monitor your time over distance and get to know your speed. Get used to the maps and navigating with them. Drink regularly through the day, and assess how many seasonal water sources are running, this will give you a good idea of what to expect ahead.

Above all, relax and enjoy this week, it is a golden time. Take the time to observe the desert environment, it is beautiful in a myriad of intricate ways.

## WEATHER AND WHEN TO HIKE

Spring through to autumn is the season for hiking and backpacking on the Pacific Crest. Winter recreation is outside of the scope of this guide, although the area offers endless opportunities for the well-prepared. Heat and snow, the two extremes, are likely to be the main considerations when planning a hike. Too early in the season and you will face challenges with cold and deep snow on higher ground, especially in the north, and in the big mountains, which become impassable without specialist equipment and techniques.

The desert lands of the first 700 miles can heat up quickly in the spring, seeing temperatures climb in excess of 100°F (38°C). In places shade is limited and exertion in such heat becomes a risk to health. Water sources will dry up and exacerbate the problem. However, start too early and the southern sections may be wet, as frontal storms drive eastward,

Spring rains bring color to the desert (Stage 1)

*The author approaching Mount Baden-Powell summit just after sunrise in May 2023 (Stage 16)*

with overnight temperatures dropping below freezing, a combination that increases the risk of hypothermia. Late March to early May are the ideal times to hike these sections, although snow could still hinder progress on Mount San Jacinto and Mount Baden-Powell.

Further north spring comes later, and snow lingers on higher ground. In most years, thru-hikers won't head into the Sierra Nevada much before mid June. Section hikers without the same time pressure might wait a couple more weeks before conditions are ideal. Too much sun here in early season is not necessarily a good thing. It will lead to rapid snow melt and run-off, leading to fast and dangerous high-water in creeks that need to be crossed.

Skipping north won't avoid snow either. Many of the trail's high points south of Oregon are above 6000ft where snow can linger, particularly on north-facing slopes. Consideration must be given to the past winter's snowpack and recent reports of local conditions. In an average year snow can remain in Northern California into late July and can cause an issue for hikers, especially on the descent from Sonora Pass, the descent from Dicks Pass in Desolation Wilderness, and in a high snow year, even on Grizzly Peak, north of Castella.

Throughout summer UV exposure can be a concern, especially at altitude where its impact is greater. As the daily hours of sunshine increase, so does evaporation. This leads to a build-up of cumulonimbus clouds that generate the afternoon thunderstorms so typical of an alpine environment. These can drop tremendous quantities of rain (or worse, hail) in a short period and often bring lightning too. Such storms are largely unavoidable, but you can respond sensibly when they happen. Endeavor to cross high passes and exposed ground early in the day. If a storm develops, consider turning back, seek lower ground, and wait it out. Lightning strikes, whether direct or nearby, can kill. Don't underestimate the risk.

Snow will typically remain a problem in Washington until early July. The sheer volume of precipitation here is higher than average. August is often the driest month for hiking. Most thru-hikers however will be here in September and can expect to receive a good deal of rain. The biggest risk here is arriving too late. The first snowfalls typically arrive by mid October. Being off trail before they happen is sensible. Snowfall in Washington is wet and heavy, creating high avalanche risk, not something you want to experience in the North Cascades where the trail often lies transverse to steep slopes.

As autumn arrives, storms occur increasingly further south too and the temperature starts dropping with them. Snowfall becomes more likely on the higher ground of north and central California across September and most hikers will want to be out of the mountains by the end of October.

It is important to remember that you will be hiking the crest of the mountains. This is high ground that catches the weather due to topography and altitude. Hikers should therefore be prepared for the possibility of unseasonal storms and even snow anywhere on the route throughout the year.

*Unexpected snow in early May in the desert! (Stage 8)*

*Wizard Island, a more recent eruption in the 'Crater Lake' of Mt. Mazama (Stage 70)*

Chief Lake from Silver Pass (Stage 35)

## GETTING THERE AND BACK

For international visitors flying into the US at the start of the hike you'll want to get to San Diego. However, many more international flights go to Los Angeles (LA) and so you are likely to find a cheaper flight for this route. Getting from LA to San Diego is easy enough. You could find a connecting flight, but there are also bus and train options and for these you will first need to get a bus downtown. Look for the LAX FlyAway bus outside each terminal. It runs every 30 minutes and takes 45 minutes across town. Many buses pick up at Union Station where you will also find Amtrak, but the main bus station is nearby. It is generally better to leave booking a return flight until you know for sure when you will be finished. If you do book a return, ensure it is flexible in case you need to return home early.

Once in San Diego, public transit buses run from downtown to Campo (with a change at El Cajon Transit Center) taking around three hours. If you travel to San Diego by bus, you might find you can get off at El Cajon on the way downtown, saving around an hour. Details at www.sdmts.com. Alternatively, you could use the privately-run PCT Southern Terminus Shuttle which picks up at the Old Town

Transit Center and will stop at REI for last minute gear purchases on the way to the Southern Terminus. They also offer camping at Camp Lockett close to the terminus. The service is considerably more expensive than the public bus but is very convenient. Details at www.pctsouthernterminusshuttle.com.

*Crossing the falls on the Cispus River headwaters below Old Snowy Mountain (Stage 88)*

Getting to and from trailheads along the trail is less easy as there is rarely public transport provision. However, the communities along the trail are aware of this and are usually very friendly and helpful to hikers, and quick to offer lifts from trailheads and common hitch-hiking spots. Of course, the outdoor community are some of the friendliest people you will ever meet (must be something to do with time spent outdoors) and most hikers out for a day hike are happy to help longer-distance hikers too.

At the Northern Terminus you are still deep in the woods. If you hike across the border into Canada and out to the highway at Manning Park, then it is possible to hitch west toward Vancouver. It is around 135 miles, or about three hours with traffic so a long hitch! It is easier to secure a 40-mile hitch as far as the town of Hope, from where you can get a bus to Vancouver several times a day. Details at www.bctransit.com. There is a private bus service from Manning Park to Vancouver that runs twice a week on Wednesdays and Saturdays. Details at www.mountainmanmikes.ca. If you don't cross into Canada, then you have around a 30-mile walk back to Hart's Pass. If you're patient, it is usually possible to find a ride from there, for the 18.6 miles of unpaved road to Mazama from where public transport is possible. Details at www.okanogantransit.com.

## PERMITS AND REGULATIONS

Hikers from international destinations will need a US visa to be in the country for between three and six months. For most this will be the 'B-2 visa'. Generally, this entails submitting a form, providing recent photos and attending an interview. You will also need a valid passport with at least six months remaining on it. There can be long wait times for interviews so schedule this well in advance of your trip. Many people worry about the interview, but it is usually very straightforward. Details at www.travel.state.gov/content/travel/en/us-visas/tourism-visit/visitor.html.

Pinchot Pass (Stage 31)

If you hope to cross into Canada from the Northern Terminus, then you will need a permit to cross the border on the PCT (even Canadians need this). Details at www.cbsa-asfc.gc.ca/travel-voyage/pecpct-eng.html. Note that it is illegal for anyone to cross into the US from Canada on the PCT corridor, so southbound hikers must start at Hart's Pass then walk to the border.

The permit system for backcountry recreation in the US can seem complex to visitors from countries where such systems aren't in place. Permits are required for some national parks, forests and wilderness areas along the PCT. However, there is no consistent approach to this. For example:

- A permit may be required for hiking, or only for overnight camping
- In some places there are quotas, others are unlimited
- Some require online reservation, others are issued when you turn up
- Some permits are free, whereas others require payment
- For some you need to visit a ranger station, others are self-service at a trailhead

Permit requirements change from year to year, so it is important to check what is required. The PCTA make this easy with the provision of an interactive map and links to all permit issuing authorities. Details at www.pcta.org/discover-the-trail/permits/local-permits. An increasing number of permits, along with campsites, can be booked through the www.recreation.gov website and app. It is useful to download this in advance. Details at www.recreation.gov/mobile-app.

If you are thru-hiking, or planning a long section, you may prefer the ease of a single long-distance permit. These are issued by the PCTA on behalf of the Forest Service. They are available for hikes over 500 miles (wherever they start) and supersede the need for local permits along the PCT corridor. You don't need a long-distance permit to undertake a long-distance hike, but it certainly makes the hike easier knowing you won't have to book or pick up permits along the way.

Long-distance permits are limited to a total of 8000 per year (in 2024), but only 4500 of these are available for northbound thru-hikes with starting points south of Sonora Pass. Because of the popularity of these among aspiring northbound thru-hikers, there is a lottery system in place. At the time of writing this required registering online in advance at www.portal.permit.pcta.org/manage/register.php. Permits are then released in two batches, with up to 50 available for each start date between March 1 and May 31. The first release of up to 35 per day usually takes place sometime in November of the prior year, followed by a second release of the remaining 15 per day in January of the hiking year.

*The moraine left by the receding Packwood Glacier with Mount Rainier behind (Stage 88)*

The lottery element comes through the randomized allocation of time slots for applications on each release date. If you are lucky, you will get an early slot and permits will be available, although not necessarily for your ideal date. In practice you just select the closest one to your ideal date as possible. If you don't get one, or get a date you're not happy with, then you get a second chance to apply (or change your date) on the second release date. If you want to hike with a partner the system allows you to link two applications and apply for a matching start date (where those permits are available).

If you're not successful getting a long-distance permit to start from the Southern Terminus, you can still hike. Apply for a long-distance permit to hike north from Sonora Pass (these are less popular), then apply for local permits where required for the sections south of Sonora Pass. In 2023 that included Cleveland National Forest (www.recreation.gov), San Jacinto Wilderness (self-issued at Idyllwild Ranger Station), and the US Forest Service for Kennedy Meadows to Sonora Pass (www.recreation.gov). In 2023 none of these local permits were limited by quota. Just be aware that the objective of the permit system

*The unassuming stone cairn outside Acton is the PCT Completion (or 'Golden Spike') Monument, dedicated in 1993 (Stage 18)*

is to limit crowding and environmental damage, so make an extra effort to travel quietly, and practice Leave No Trace principles.

One final permit that everyone must have, is the California Campfire permit. These are free and unlimited. They just require you to complete some online training on the safety and management of campfires. Details at: www.readyforwildfire.org/permits.

## WAYMARKING AND NAVIGATION

The PCT is a well-marked trail that is not difficult to follow. That can be a problem as a lot of hikers don't take it seriously, and don't carry anything other than a phone for navigating. There are unmarked junctions, eroded areas where the trail is unclear, and at times it will be buried under snow. All hikers will leave the trail too, for the bathroom, to find water and to camp. These are the times when it is most easy to get 'turned around' and be unsure of the way back to the trail. It doesn't take a lot to get a bit lost and it is important to know how to 'relocate' yourself.

With the use of GPS apps on smartphones, this is usually as easy as following the arrow, however if a phone is lost or broken (a surprisingly common occurrence) then it is challenging without a map and compass. Following a map is not hard provided you use a compass to check where north is and orient the map by turning it so that the top points north, then the map layout matches the ground. A button compass is sufficient, is tiny and weighs almost nothing. Many sports watches also have a compass that will suffice.

Following where you are on an actual map (as opposed to checking the dot on a digital map) is not only good practice but also builds your skill at relating your environment to the map, helping you to understand the landscape features coming up,

*A sagebrush lizard enjoys a viewpoint near Lake Hughes (Stage 20)*

and recognizing them when they do. This practice will build your confidence in the outdoors and competence with navigating. Anyone undertaking a thru-hike has enough time outdoors to become a very competent navigator and this will enable you to design your own routes in the future, away from the signposted trails.

The number of maps required for the PCT adds too much weight for most hikers, even when carried a few at a time. The map booklets in this guide are carefully designed at a scale of 1:100,000 to provide you with enough detail to understand the landscape around you, to check in and follow your progress, monitor your time over distance and help you to relocate yourself if you need to. They will provide a back-up to a phone app and are a useful tool to develop your navigation skills without adding much weight. They are not a substitute for more detailed maps in poor conditions, such as snow.

*Ericameria linearfolia (or Goldenbush) is a common sight in the California deserts (Stage 22)*

*Americorps trail crew work to repair trail damage in Whitewater Canyon (Stage 9)*

## WATER SUPPLY

Collecting water from creeks, springs, lakes or dubious plastic bottles left at a cache by the side of the trail by a stranger, may seem a questionable practice to those not yet initiated into the world of backpacking, but (with the exception of the plastic bottles) this is how mankind has collected water for millennia. Piped water, and especially bottled water, is quite a modern phenomenon. For most there is considerable anxiety about the purity of water collected from natural sources. It is true that there are bacteria, amoeba, parasites and viruses sometimes found in water that can make you quite sick. However, in the mountains especially, it is not as big a problem as some would have you believe.

Water from mountain springs, and in the small creeks higher up, that carry fast-flowing water down hillsides is most likely to be uncontaminated. The lower, and slower, water gets, the more chance there is that it has become contaminated. Water that has joined larger rivers, or passed through lakes has a higher chance of contamination. In areas such as meadows and plains, where cattle graze, contamination becomes very likely.

The age-old approach to dealing with this problem, is to boil the water. Simply bringing it to the boil will neutralize most things, including the *Giardia* organism. A rolling boil for several minutes is the gold-standard for purity. However, all that boiling requires fuel, which is

*A water cache left on a desert road crossing – always filter water taken from a cache (Stage 24)*

Long stretches of trail are waterless in Angeles National Forest (Stage 19)

heavy. In our modern age there are much better, lightweight solutions to the problem. Chemical disinfectants in the form of tablets or drops are lightweight and effective against most micro-organisms. Purifiers using UV light are very effective but a little heavier as they require batteries. They also need careful handling in case they become broken. Most hikers will carry a filtration-based system, of which there are several on the market. These are reasonably affordable, lightweight, reliable, and effective. The one downside is perhaps that some can be a little slow to use. They can become clogged too and it is worth becoming familiar with back-flushing and cleaning them.

Of course, any of these systems will only work effectively if you scrupulously ensure that not even a drop of the untreated water finds its way to the treated water, container, utensils or food. This seems obvious, but does require considerable care in collection and treatment.

## FOOD AND RESUPPLY

There are a number of approaches to food and resupply on any long trail. These include:

- Take a chance and buy what you can along the way
- Package up all resupply boxes in advance and send them ahead
- Adopt a feast and famine approach: eat well in towns and then snack in between
- Send resupply boxes from bigger trail towns to smaller places in each section

There is no right way and hikers have tried each of these strategies. Mailing boxes gets expensive quickly, but for some hikers with specific dietary requirements it is useful to know they'll have what they need. In addition to the cost, mailing ahead also ties you to the post office or other business opening hours. In recent years a lot of the small stores close to the PCT have realized the opportunity, and now try to stock what hikers generally want. If you are flexible about what you eat, you can hike most of the trail relying just on what you can buy on route. Unless your daily mileage is quite low you can usually resupply every four to five days and only a couple of times might you need to carry 7 to 10 days' of food.

In practice it is most common for hikers to pick up most of their food in the small stores, and occasionally markets in larger towns that can be accessed from the trail, then to supplement this with a few small boxes

Red Tahquitz ridgeline below Mount San Jacinto (Stage 7)

sent, from trail towns to the handful of places where choice could be quite limited. Some hikers will use a 'bounce-box' to forward some spares, town clothes and other items they may want sporadically ahead, sending it each time to the next place they may want it. If you do this then it is easy to add some food into it when you are in a town, for wherever up the trail you may need it. If you use a USPS Priority Mailing Box for this, you have the option to 'bounce' it to another post office without charge if you don't need it yet.

What you choose to eat is down to a combination of personal preference, availability, and weight. Dried or dehydrated foods are the lightest. Of course, water needs adding at the preparation stage and there are two approaches to this. Using a stove for cooking, or cold-soaking. Canister gas is widely available along the trail these days. Liquid and solid fuel stoves without a shut-off valve often can't be used due to fire bans across the summer. Sooner or later many hikers experiment with cold-soaking. It is simple and quite effective. Add water to food, in a tub with a lid, at lunchtime, and it is ready to eat when you arrive at camp.

Mount Thielsen is known as one of Oregon's 'Matterhorns' (Stage 71)

Commercially prepared backpacking meals are an option. Some are great, others less so, but they are expensive, so rarely an option for longer trips. Pasta, rice, powdered potato, couscous and noodles are likely to form the base of most meals. Dried summer sausage, cheese and tuna (foil packets not tins) are common proteins. Vegetables and salad can be a challenge. Dehydrated vegetables do turn up in a few stores. Always carry a few fresh things from each resupply for the first day or two and eat healthy produce in town whenever you can. Oats and granola are good options that travel well. Tortilla wraps aren't too heavy and can be filled with all sorts from peanut butter to potato chips. Snack bars, protein bars and other 'instant' wrapped foods are useful. Trail mix is a great way to get some more healthy protein, fats and fibre too. It's important to recognize that your diet won't always be ideal, so consider a

*The definition of Trail Magic: a complete stranger pulls in at Walker Pass trailhead with fresh pizza and cold water (Stage 25)*

multi-vitamin supplement, and don't forget electrolytes either.

It is at trailheads, or on the way to town for resupply that you are most likely to encounter Trail Angels. These are generous individuals who go out of their way to help and support people under-taking long hikes on the PCT. They might offer food, offer you rides to/from town, offer you accommodation, or help in other ways. When this is offered freely without expectation of reward, it is known as Trail Magic. In appropriate cases do offer a small donation, whatever you can afford, to help the Trail Angel to help others. This used to be known as 'paying it forward'. With the growing number of hikers on the trail, things are changing and there are now more people seeing this as an opportunity and 'requiring' donations. When this happens, they are offering a service commercially, but informally, for reward. If you are ever uncomfortable with this, or the level of 'donation', ask for a receipt before proceeding, or decline.

## CAMPING

In this guide the term 'tent site' has been used to describe ground that has been previously cleared (usually by previous hikers) to place a tent. There are no facilities, fences, or signs. A campsite or campground on the other hand is a recognized camping area designated as such by the relevant authorities, and usually having some basic facilities, such as picnic tables and firepits, for some even an outhouse/toilet.

On the PCT you should try to camp in existing tent sites where possible to prevent further damage to ground shrubs and plants. The ground can be quite stony in places, sometimes sandy too. This can be quite hard on tents, and it is worth carrying a light ground sheet to protect your tent floor from damage. When the weather is fine you may want to consider 'cowboy camping' without a tent, in which case a ground sheet will help to protect your sleeping pad.

When you choose a site, look around and consider any hazards or the effect of the conditions. It is helpful to be sure you don't pitch on ant nest for example, or near nesting bees. Look up too and be wary of dead trees or dead-looking branches

*Trail-side camp in the San Gabriel Mountains (Stage 16)*

*Larger tent sites can be quite social as hikers meet up and compare notes (Stage 2)*

that could fall in a breeze. Don't camp close to water either, creeks or lakes will increase air moisture leading to condensation in your tent. Condensation is also likely on clear nights when warm air cools rapidly creating dew, then having your tent tucked in among trees and shrubs can help avoid condensation. If rain is possible ensure it will flow away from your tent not under it. You don't want to wake up in a pool!

It is good practice to cook and prepare food away from your tent as this will minimize your chance of unwanted wildlife encounters, not only bears, but rodents will happily chew through your pack to reach food. If you keep all food and other scented items sealed away, and your gear and camp clean, then you will be left alone. In several places on the PCT you are now required to store food and scented items in a hard-sided bear canister. There is a growing argument that it is worth carrying one for the whole trail. They do make a handy stool to sit on too.

Finally, toilet hygiene! Always walk well away from the trail, water sources and tent or camp sites to toilet. Carry a small trowel and ensure that deposits are buried at least six inches deep. Never cover with rocks as animals soon uncover this, and always pack out toilet paper. It is the only way to ensure it doesn't end up littering the landscape.

## EQUIPMENT

In choosing equipment you will always be making compromises. Lightweight is generally better, but not always. Every ounce (or gram) that you carry will put a strain on your body and feet, and will need to be carried up every mountain on trail. However, you will quickly regret not having a warm layer or gloves if you are stuck on the side of a snowy mountain developing hypothermia. So, you are making choices between comfort while hiking versus comfort in camp, and safety if you, or the conditions deteriorate.

With modern lightweight gear, it is possible to be safe and comfortable without carrying excessive loads. Keep things as light as you can but be wary of getting caught up in the race to gain kudos from the lightest pack, it can backfire.

*Sunset in Granite Chief Wilderness (Stage 43)*

## Camping and carrying

Often referred to as the 'big three', your pack (or rucksack), tent and sleeping system will be your heaviest items. You should aim to keep each of these below about 2.2lbs (1kg). A pack of around 50–65 litres is usually about right. Remember that at times, as much as half the volume and weight of your pack will be food and water. Consider whether a vented back panel is important to you and whether the load transfers effectively to the hip belt. Comfort is as important as weight. Consider how you will carry a bear canister too, inside or strapped on. You will need a pack liner to protect from moisture, but a refuse sack will suffice.

Shelter options are varied but the main debate is between free-standing tents versus trekking-pole tents. The latter assumes of course that you are already carrying trekking poles. Using trekking poles for support in place of dedicated poles saves weight and these tents are invariably lighter. However, on stony ground freestanding tents have an obvious advantage not needing to be pegged out. There are too few trees on several trail sections for hammocks to be a viable option on the PCT.

Sleeping quilts are often chosen over bags due to the weight savings but can be more susceptible to drafts. Down is preferable to synthetic insulation, but it must be kept dry, or it will lose its insulating properties. A liner is useful and will keep your bag or quilt much cleaner. Silk is generally lightest. The warmth rating is a very personal choice. Many hikers will want a bag/quilt rated down to 20°F (-6.6°C), but if you sleep cold, you may want a lower-rated bag.

Sleeping mat choices range from simple closed cell foam to insulated inflatable mats with warmth ratings like sleeping bags. Side-sleepers will invariably want an inflatable mat for comfort. Consider both weight and durability when choosing: if you are thru-hiking it will get a lot of abuse.

## Cooking and hydration

You will need a means of purifying water, and options are discussed in more detail in the Water supply section. You'll also need the capacity to carry several litres of water. Soft bottles are better to save space when not in use. As mentioned in Food and resupply, canister gas stoves are now the most common type, and gas is available in most places. A small titanium pot that doubles as a cup (750ml is most common), and a spoon are all you really need. A supply of zip-seal bags is useful as you will frequently re-package food to save space. If you want to cold soak, then a pot with a lid will be needed instead. You will need a bear canister beyond Kennedy Meadows South. There are several varieties of hard-sided canisters. Soft-sided bear-proof sacks aren't accepted as adequate in some areas.

South Fork Kern River in South Sierra Wilderness (Stage 28)

## Hiking and navigating

Trekking poles offer a lot of benefits, enabling you to use four limbs to make progress and steady yourself, rather than just two. Using your arms assists considerably in moving you and your pack uphill, and in descent reduces the strain on your knees as well as protecting against a trip or fall. They are especially valuable during creek crossings for stability in fast flowing water. If you choose a trekking pole tent, then they also form the structure of your shelter.

As mentioned in Waymarking and navigation, a compass is invaluable, however small. Combined with a basic map you become freed from phone/GPS app dependency. Be aware that dedicated trail apps offer a view of the trail corridor, but rarely the wider area. Try to download the GPX tracks onto a fully featured GPS app in case you need to navigate far off trail, say in the event of a fire closure.

## Clothing

Clothing should work together as a system so that you can layer up, if necessary, when cold. Modern synthetics or merino wool are best. Avoid cotton which doesn't dry well. Check that synthetics are treated to prevent odour build-up. Your fellow hikers will thank you!

*Deep snow on Mount San Jacinto slows progress considerably (Stage 8)*

Outside of the shoulder seasons, for most, shorts will be your primary legwear. Keep them loose for comfort and layering. Running tights or warmer long-johns are great for camp, cold nights or layered under shorts on cold days. Some shorts include a liner, but separate underwear is better. Ensure it is breathable, dries quickly and doesn't chafe. Wool socks should be well-fitting and durable. Some hikers swear by Injinji toe-socks. You only need two pairs of underwear and socks, one to wear and one to rinse out (ideally daily).

Sun hoodies have become popular for the upper body, and many have thumb loops to protect the back of your hands from sun. Some hikers however still prefer traditional hiking shirts. In the shoulder seasons you may want a mid-layer such as a light fleece. A duvet jacket is the preferred insulation for cold evenings, and you'll want a second base-layer to change into in camp too.

Waterproofs are essential as a wind barrier as much as for rain. You won't wear them a lot, but when you do, you'll be glad of them. Finally, consider your extremities. You'll need a hat that also protects your neck and ears unless you're using a hoodie, then a baseball cap is fine. On cold nights and mornings, you'll also want a woolly hat, especially if you have a sleeping quilt without a built-in hood. Don't forget your hands. Sun gloves if you don't have a top with thumb loops, and a warmer pair. If you get cold hands then also take a pair of simple, shell rain mitts as a wind and rain barrier.

### Footwear

Few hikers will use heavy boots on the PCT. Walking shoes and trail running shoes are lighter, more flexible and enable you to move more freely. They are not as durable however, and a thru-hike might see you replace them as many as five times. Consider adding a better-quality insole with enough arch support. This can really help minimize overuse injuries. You will want well-vented shoes, large enough to allow your feet to expand, which they will in the desert heat especially.

Many hikers will use small nylon gaiters designed for use with trail runners to keep debris out of their shoes. To some this will seem unnecessary but consider that every bit of fine dust and grit that works its way into your shoes will mix with sweat and rub, both your skin and socks, causing wear and potentially leading to blisters.

*Boiling Springs Lake in Lassen Volcanic National Park (Stage 49)*

Tributary of Fish Creek in spate (Stage 35)

Some hikers also carry camp footwear such as Crocs or flipflops. This is very much a personal choice. They're certainly nice to have, but shouldn't be used for creek crossing unless they are very secure.

## Electronics

For most hikers, their phone is also their camera, notebook, GPS and more. It gets a lot of use and will need charging, so you'll want a charging block, for two-pin US outlets (ideally with folding pins), relevant connector cables and a lightweight USB backup battery for intermediate charges between towns. Portable solar panels are an option but can be heavy. If you have a smartwatch, include a cable for that too. You'll need a small, lightweight headtorch, many of these can also be charged by USB which is more convenient than carrying spare conventional batteries.

Many hikers will carry a Personal Locator Beacon (PLB) for safety. These require a subscription to access the satellite network and regular charging. If keeping in touch with family is important, then several offer a satellite messaging service too.

## Hygiene

A bandana or other small cloth is useful for washing (always take water away from the source to avoid pollution). You should not take soap products into the backcountry. Consider

*Hiker walking the LA Aqueduct through the Mojave Desert section (Stage 21)*

decanting any cream or moisturizer into small re-fillable tubs. A toilet trowel is essential. You won't need a full-size towel. Consider cutting a travel towel down to about a 12-inch square. There are different challenges for all genders on trail. Some hikers may wish to purchase a Kula Cloth, a reusable, anti-microbial pee cloth that prevents the need for copious amounts of toilet tissue. Any sanitary products used must be packed out, but there are alternatives, including silicone/menstrual cups and discs. There are many blogs to read with advice on this topic, but ultimately it is down to personal discretion.

### Miscellaneous

Other items not covered above include reading glasses or contact lenses if you need them. You'll want good sunglasses too, not only in bright sun, but also in snow which can be blinding. Many hikers use a bum bag/fanny pack to keep snacks and small items close to hand while hiking. A neck buff is a useful extra when cold but can also serve as pillowcase around a filled dry bag, or even an emergency bandage. Umbrellas are growing in popularity, especially against the desert sun but are a nice item to have in rain too. If you need to deal with snow and ice in the higher mountains, then microspikes or crampons will be needed, and possibly an ice axe. At some point you will also want a mosquito head net and some repellent. Finally, a basic first aid kit to deal with common issues.

*The skeletal remains of a Whitebark Pine tree – the oldest living one in the park is estimated at 500 years old (Stage 70)*

Helen Lake, below Muir Pass (Stage 33)

## HEALTH AND FIRST AID

The health issues most common on the PCT are blisters, sprains, small cuts and gastrointestinal problems. Serious injuries are rare. A basic first aid kit should be able to deal with these issues. Improvisation can be used to manage a lot of things with a little know-how. It is highly recommended you attend a first aid course before setting out.

Stomach complaints are often blamed on bad food or water but are more often due to poor hygiene. Washing regularly and generally keeping clean goes a long way toward remaining healthy. Be mindful not to eat directly after toileting. Rubbing moist foliage in your hands is quite effective as a hand cleanser. Carry and use sterilizing wipes on broken skin such as cuts or blisters to prevent infections.

## HAZARDS AND SAFETY

People's perception of danger on the PCT commonly includes meeting bears, snakes, spiders, a mountain lion, or bad people. These are rarely

*Mica Lake, north of Glacier Peak (Stage 96)*

the real risks. Simple habits protect against these. Keep food and scented items wrapped and protected and never disturb a bear with cubs. It's very rare to see a mountain lion. If you do, face it, don't run and it will soon leave. Rattlesnakes will bathe in the sun and usually retreat if they are aware of you. Be attentive in higher risk areas, bites only happen if you stand on or very near one. Don't put your hands/fingers in holes in the ground, trees, rocks, or old buildings.

Plants pose a greater problem than animals, particularly if you have an allergy. Poison oak is a shrub common under oak trees, particularly in southern California. Poodle-dog bush is a mountain shrub with purple flowers and a pungent smell that thrives in recent burn areas. Both can cause anything from a mild rash to severe respiratory distress.

*Crossing Cottonwood creek in flood (Stage 2)*

Mosquitos tend to emerge for a couple of weeks after the snow recedes, so later as you head further north. They can be a nuisance. Treat clothing in advance with permethrin, use a repellent and have a head net for the occasions (usually evening) when they are bad. These actions will keep any ticks at bay too.

People around the trail are almost universally friendly, but when you hitchhike exercise caution. If something feels off, or sets off alarm bells, pass up the ride and wait, another ride will always come along, and another hiker may join you. Often the greater risk to health and safety is you. When you are in the backcountry away from access to help, always take extra care. Self-inflicted injuries are commonly caused by tripping, careless foot placement, jumping off rocks or logs and careless use of knives.

The biggest risk to life comes from creek crossings. If you're ever unsure, wait for others, wait for lower water in the morning when snow-melt has slowed, or find another crossing point, either upstream where tributaries are smaller, or downstream where the water is wider and slower.

The Devils Postpile National Monument (Stage 36)

## LANDSCAPE AND GEOLOGY

The PCT is very varied, passing through six of the US's seven eco-zones: alpine tundra, subalpine forest, upper montane forest, lower montane forest, upper Sonoran (oak woodlands and grassland), and lower Sonoran (the Mojave and Sonoran Deserts). Underneath all this the forces of continental drift and plate tectonics have crafted a craggy spine of ridges and mountains, part of the Pacific 'Ring of Fire'. The foothills of southern California and mountains of the Sierra Nevada formed from slowly cooling magma, allowing the coarse grains of granite to form with subsequent erosion contributing to the sandy, gravely ground we see today.

North of Sonora Pass, in Central California, the granite gives way to predominantly volcanic rock with sporadic granite outcrops which underlie many of the lakes of the region. Metamorphic rock such as the limestone of Marble Mountain Wilderness makes an appearance here too. The picture is complicated somewhat by the San Andreas Fault which has shifted some rocks as far as 200 miles north-west. In places magma remains close to the surface creating the hot springs found in Deep Creek in San Bernardino National

Eagle Rock is a rock formation close to Warner Springs (Stage 5)

Forest, and in the heart of Lassen Volcanic National Park.

From Lassen Peak the Cascade Mountains gain in stature through Oregon and across Washington and the landscape is obviously volcanic. A showcase of volcanic forms, the area is still active with lava flows as young as 200 years old. Tall conical mountains such as Mount Shasta are stratovolcanos, these are often surrounded by smaller cinder cones. Lava domes, such as Lassen Peak, build from highly viscous lava, whereas shield volcanos with low viscosity lava are responsible for the huge lava fields that can travel for miles. In the north the effects of recent glaciation can be seen with active glaciers present on many peaks including Mount Adams, Mount Rainer and Glacier Peak.

## PLANTS AND FLOWERS

The desert in bloom is one of the highlights of the trail, especially if you happen to start early. It is not the barren rock and sand that many might imagine. Oak, fir and pine trees line the creek beds and gullies (sometimes with poison oak lurking below) while scrub oak, ceanothus and manzanita spread out across the hillsides. Pockets of color emerge as poppies and penstemon burst forth, and lupines reach for the sky. In the San Felipe Valley and Tehachapi Mountains, you might spot the classic desert cholla and prickly pear cacti as well as plenty of creosote bush scrub. In the northern desert sections the Mojave yucca and Joshua trees climb out of barren ground.

The change is gradual as you climb into the Sierra Nevada. Juniper and pine multiply in number as do the woody shrubs. Most of California's alpine flora are perennial herbs, some of which are considered relic plants that survived the last ice age. In the alpine zone adaptation to the harsh environment has created dense mats of miniature shrubs knotted together

*Poodle-dog bush is common, especially in recently burned areas. It can cause significant irritation (Stage 19)*

Sierra tiger lilies alongside the trail (Stage 61)

in protection against the elements. Relics can be found in Northern California too, among the lodgepole pine and mountain spirea; look carefully in seeps and gullies, and you might find the carnivorous California pitcher plant.

In Oregon, the hiker would be forgiven for perceiving the flora as, perhaps a bit boring. It can seem as though the somewhat flatter trail winds through endless homogenous forest. Look a little closer and you realize there is great diversity, indeed the diversity of conifer trees alone here is greater than anywhere else in the world. The difference is that plant communities here tend to co-exist, rather than each occupying unique ecological niches as they tend to where there is greater elevation change. As you enter Washington this pattern begins to change again. The moisture-laden temperate rainforest holds much denser communities of flora. Wildflowers are here in abundance, overflowing the trail and drenching you below the knee when wet. For many hikers their favourite feature of Washington's flora might be the abundance of huckleberries and thimbleberries, invariably ready to eat in September. Just remember, you are sharing them with the bears!

## WILDLIFE

The wildlife of the PCT corridor changes as you hike north, just as the landscape and the flora does, as part of each interconnected and often over-lapping ecological system. The picture is complex, and you will only see a fraction of the species whose habitat you will walk through. According to the US Geological Survey, there are 175 species of mammals, 75 species of reptiles, 50 species of amphibians and 315 species of birds on the PCT corridor alone. That doesn't even include the tens of thousands of arachnid and insect species that include spiders, beetles, flies, butterflies, moths, ants, bees and wasps. It is truly a living landscape.

For many the memorable encounters will be with the larger creatures, or those that have the potential to be dangerous such as the black bear (it can be a variety of colors), the mountain lion (also known as a cougar or puma), or the rattlesnake. Perhaps more enchanting are the mule deer that will graze around the tents of sleeping hikers. Coyotes will more likely be heard than seen, howling, and yipping in groups in the evening.

Walk late into darkness, especially in southern California and you might spot a scorpion exploring the trail. A sting would be quite unpleasant but wouldn't kill. Other nocturnal visitors include the bushy-tailed woodrat and the brush mouse. Along with the golden-mantled ground squirrel and the yellow-pine chipmunk these persistent scavengers will make short work of any food scraps, indeed they'll raid your food bag if they can get into it.

The higher elevations hold their own special creature delights. It would be hard to miss the comical yellow-bellied marmots, especially when sitting high on a rock emitting a piercing whistle. However, the source of the more fearful squeak, usually emanating from boulder fields near the high passes will require a harder look. Movement usually gives away the cute little pika as it scurries beneath its rock sanctuary. And fearful it has reason to be, for these skies among the big mountains are where you're most likely to see the golden and bald eagles – and if you're fortunate perhaps the rare California condor, but more likely its common cousin the turkey vulture.

*A Long-nosed Leopard Lizard, south of Tehachapi*

*Hikers share the trail with a rich diversity of wildlife*

## LEAVE NO TRACE

Leave No Trace is a set of ethics promoting conservation of the outdoors. While the concept started as a movement in the United States in response to ecological damage caused by wilderness recreation, it has grown into a set of principles recognized worldwide in particular relation to human use of the natural environment for recreation.

As more of us seek out the experience of the natural world for rest and recreation we risk damaging and degrading the very environment we come to enjoy. Leave No Trace principles draw our attention to the risks, and help us to identify and to reduce the impact we have.

I would encourage everyone planning to hike the PCT to visit the PCTA website section on Leave No Trace principles; there are lots of things you can do to protect the environment and the trail. However, the basics are simple and include the following:

- Hike on the trail, never cut switchbacks or trample delicate plants
- Camp on durable surfaces, don't damage trees or build structures
- Toilet at least 200ft from water sources and campsites, in a hole at least six inches deep
- Carry a trowel for digging and a waste bag to pack out toilet paper (don't bury or burn it)
- Pack out ALL waste, including anything biodegradable (orange peel and banana skins too!)
- Don't light campfires unless you really need one, too many wildfires start this way!
- Protect wildlife by protecting all food and scented products, ideally in a bear canister
- Respect others, be friendly and maintain the peace and quiet for all

### THE SEVEN LEAVE NO TRACE PRINCIPLES

- Plan ahead and prepare
- Travel and camp on durable surfaces
- Dispose of waste properly
- Leave what you find
- Minimize campfire impacts
- Respect wildlife
- Be considerate of other visitors

Mount Rainier from Goat Rocks ridge (Stage 88)

*A hiker pauses to take in the view across the Laguna Mountains (Stage 3)*

## USING THIS GUIDE

The trail divides naturally into five regions, and at a steady pace each of these takes around a month to cross. These have been divided into 11 sections to provide hikes of between two and three weeks each. A further subdivision breaks these into 100 smaller stages of between one and three days each. Where possible these stages end at road trailheads, but on occasion they end at trail junctions from where it is possible to hike out to a road.

The guide has been presented as three booklets to enable the hiker to keep the weight they carry to the absolute minimum, while still carrying a physical guide and maps that can both supplement, and if necessary, replace a digital mapping app.

Each of the 11 sections starts with an overview map of the route covered. This is followed by a summary table of the section, showing the stages, mileage, timing, ascent and descent, a brief description and details of permits required and facilities available on the route.

The route maps are presented at 1:100,000 scale, sufficient to navigate from topography and major features most of the time. Smaller details that might be required to navigate in poor conditions will not be present. This

*Sunrise looking east from Spitler Peak on the climb to Mount San Jacinto (Stage 7)*

scale was chosen as the optimum balance between weight and detail. You will get the most out of the mapping if you follow your progress on it regularly and practice interpreting the landscape features.

Mapping is continuous throughout each booklet, and mileage is given cumulatively from 0–2655. This enables quick cross-referencing to other sources of information about conditions at any given point on trail, such as water or fire reports. Be aware that mileage will vary to a small degree from source to source as annual small changes in trail routing are updated at different times in each source.

Stage timings are indicative only, and do not include breaks. Individuals will hike faster or slower than the suggested timings. Monitor how long early stages take you against these times and use this to interpret how long future stages are likely to take you.

Stage information is overlayed on the relevant map page, with numbered map symbols marking the stage start and finish on the map. Stage summary information is given including the distance, indicative duration, total ascent and descent for the stage, and a stage profile is also provided. An introductory paragraph in each stage provides a combination of descriptive and useful information about the stage. Stage waypoints are then given with their mileage point and indicative stage timing. Waypoints do not include every junction or feature. They serve two purposes:

*Approaching a pass on old snow in Marble Mountain Wilderness (Stage 60)*

- To provide confirmation of direction at unmarked or less clear junctions
- To break the stage into regular 'checkpoints' that enable progress to be measured against indicative timings

Finally, where space allows without obscuring helpful map detail, 'fact' boxes have been overlayed to provide interesting context about the landscape, history, people, flora or fauna of the area you are passing through.

*Banner Peak above Thousand Island Lake, Ansel Adams Wilderness (Stage 36)*

## AN IMPORTANT NOTE ABOUT WATER

The strength and sometimes position of water sources can vary greatly from year to year. A great deal of effort has been made to survey the mapped water sources on the ground, as well as to validate them with historical data and other sources, but few can be relied upon absolutely. Smaller sources will wither and dry out across the summer. In a drier year these will be gone earlier, and some may never appear. Water caches should never be relied upon. They are the actions of well-meaning and independent individuals who may stop at any time.

The PCT Water Report is an invaluable crowd-sourced project managed by volunteers. It provides updates regarding water sources, fires, passes, and fords. You can access it at www.pctwater.com, on Instagram @pctwater, or on Facebook. You can also download it in several formats for offline use. Please contribute updates whenever you can.

*Mount Shasta from Castle Crags State Park (Stage 56)*

# APPENDIX A

*Local information and conversions*

Emergency telephone number
911

## Sales tax

Prices shown in shops are not the prices you pay for the goods. Sales tax will be added at the register to your final bill.

## Federal holidays

Most federal employees will be on holiday on the following dates during the hiking season. Post offices will be closed and mail will not be moved or sorted so can be disrupted for several days.

- Last Monday in May: Memorial Day
- July 4: Independence Day (or July 3 or 5, if July 4 falls during a weekend)
- First Monday in September: Labor Day
- Second Monday in October: Columbus Day

## American units conversions

1 mile = 1.6km

1000ft = 305m

1ft = 30.5cm

1in = 2.5cm

1 pint (US) = 0.5 litre

1 gallon (US) = 3.78 litres

1 pound (lb) = 0.45kg

32°F = 0°C

70°F = 21°C

100°F = 38°C

In the US feet tends to be the commonly used unit for distance rather than the yard (3ft = 1yd).

The instructions with some freeze-dried foods give quantities in terms of cups (1 cup = 240ml)

## Telephone dialling codes

The US and Canada have an integrated telephone system. To call the US or Canada from most European countries dial 001 followed by the local telephone number. To call abroad from the US or Canada, you must first dial the exit code 011, to let the carrier know it is an international call, followed by the country code. For example, the UK country code is 44.

# APPENDIX B

*Useful websites*

www.pcta.org
Pacific Crest Trail Association

www.pctwater.com
PCT Water report: crowd-sourced in-year updates on water sources, fires, passes and snow

www.readyforwildfire.org/permits
California campfire permits

www.recreation.gov
US government central reservation and permit portal (download the app!)

www.cbsa-asfc.gc.ca/travel-voyage/pecpct-eng.html
Canadian Border Services Agency PCT entry permit

www.planyourhike.com
Hike planning website with gear, food and resupply advice

www.postholer.com
Trip planner, elevation profiles, weather forecasting and the famed snow conditions report

www.pctsouthernterminusshuttle.com
The southern terminus shuttle bus

www.faroutguides.com
Provider of trail navigation apps

www.pctmap.net
PCT maps and GPS data

www.fs.usda.gov/pct
US Forest Service PCT page

www.fs.usda.gov/main/pct/maps-publications
US Forest Service PCT maps

www.trailjournals.com
Hosting site for trail journals

www.halfwayanywhere.com/pacific-crest-trail
Annual PCT hiker survey

# APPENDIX C

## *Other publications*

There are a wide range of books available written about the PCT, from guides, maps and photobooks to memoirs of every description. Hiking the PCT can be an introspective and life-changing experience and it is no surprise that people want to share that experience. There is no intent for this list to be comprehensive, but a few recommended books include the following:

*Journeys North: The Pacific Crest Trail*, Barney Scout Mann, 2020, Mountaineers Books, ISBN: 978-1680513219

*Thirst: 2600 Miles to Home*, Heather 'Anish' Anderson, 2019, Mountaineers Books, ISBN: 978-1680512366

*The Pacific Crest Trail: Exploring America's Wilderness Trail*, Mark Larabee, Barney 'Scout' Mann, 2016, Rizzoli, ISBN: 978-0847849765

*Rattlesnakes and Bald Eagles: Hiking The Pacific Crest Trail*, Chris Townsend, 2014 Sandstone Press, ISBN: 978-1908737731

*Hikertrash: Life on the Pacific Crest Trail*, Erin Miller, 2014, Erin Miller Books, ISBN: 978-0692341384

*Wild: From Lost to Found on the Pacific Crest Trail*, Cheryl Strayed, 2013, Vintage Books, ISBN: 978-0307476074

*The Last Englishman: Hiking 2,650 miles on the Pacific Crest Trail*, Keith Foskett, 2012, CreateSpace Independent Publishing Platform, ISBN: 978-1105213090

*Pacific Crest Trail Hiker's Handbook: Innovative Techniques and Trail Tested Instruction for the Long Distance Hiker*, Ray Jardine, 1996, AdventureLore Press, ISBN: 978-0963235923

*The High Adventure of Eric Ryback: Canada to Mexico on Foot*, Eric Ryback, 1971, Chronicle Books, ISBN: 978-0553023923

### Reference

*Field Guide to the Cascades and Olympics*, 2nd Ed, Rob Sandelin (Author), Stephen R Whitney (Illustrator), 2004, Mountaineers Books, ISBN: 978-0898868081

*National Geographic Field Guide to the Birds of North America*, 7th Ed, Jon L. Dunn and Jonathan Alderfur, 2017, National Geographic Society, ISBN: 978-1426218354

*The Laws Field Guide to the Sierra Nevada*, John Muir Laws, 2007, Heyday Books, ISBN: 978-1597140522

# APPENDIX D

*Schedules for planning 110- to 180-day thru-hikes*

*Looking west across Rock Creek Basin in Golden Trout Wilderness (Stage 28)*

The tables below include many of the most common or nearest resupply points to the trail as an example for the purposes of planning. They show the distance and time between these resupply points based on a moderate average pace that most hikers should easily achieve. They also show the cumulative distance and time as you progress along the trail. There are two columns for each of the 110-day plan, the 120-day, the 130-day and so on. These are the numbered day and date at which you must leave each resupply point to remain on track with that schedule.

These schedules are calculated assuming an 'average' snow year. In such a year, June 15 is about the right

**WHAT IS AN AVERAGE SNOW YEAR?**

To monitor the snow level for your year and understand whether it is above or below average, go to www.postholer.com/snow/Pacific-Crest-Trail/1 and look for the chart entitled 'Pacific Crest Trail, Sierra – SWE By Date All Year – Mile 762 to 945'. The thick black line shows an historical average, look at the line for your year by comparison to determine whether it is above or below. Check back regularly across the early part of the year and watch how the trend progresses.

*The ridgeline of Goat Rocks, a spectacular traverse with Mount Rainier ahead (Stage 88)*

*Waking to overnight snow in Castle Crags State Park (Stage 56)*

time to leave Kennedy Meadows South and head into the Sierra Nevada. Hence each schedule starts from the Southern Terminus on a different date in order to be at Kennedy Meadows South for June 15. If the year you hike is looking like an above or below average year for the Sierra section then simply adjust the schedule forward or backward by an appropriate number of days.

At the bottom of each column the averages are provided. So, for example at the foot of the columns for the 140-day schedule, you can see that, at the assumed average speed of 2.18 miles per hour, you would need to walk for approximately 8hr 42min to cover an average of 19 miles each day. The schedules do not represent a continuous pace of 2.18mph, only an average. The timings between each waypoint throughout the route are adjusted for ascent, descent, and to some degree the terrain. This is based on the collective experience from five thru-hikes by this and the previous author of this guide. It cannot accurately represent the conditions that you may face as these do change a little from year to year, for example in 2023 there was a lot of avalanche damage and trail erosion after the record snowfall earlier that year.

The tables do not include any zero days. You may want to have some shorter days too. In practice you will be likely to walk faster than 2.18mph once you are fit. Most hikers with light to moderate weight packs will build up to walking around 2.6mph on average. If you pick a schedule that is not too ambitious, then build up your fitness, you will find that you can easily afford to have a few low mileage days when you leave trail to resupply, without affecting your schedule. The best way to approach zero days is to 'earn' them. If you are walking well and comfortable, add a couple of miles onto each day and build up a 'buffer' that you can 'spend' on a restful zero once in a while.

**Table 1** Schedules for 110-, 120-, 130- and 140-day thru-hikes

| Section | Resupply Point | Mile | Mile Cum | hr:min | Hr Cum |
|---|---|---|---|---|---|
| | Southern Terminus | 0 | 0 | 0 | 0 |
| | Mount Laguna | 41.5 | 41.5 | 19:30 | 19:30 |
| 1 | Warner Springs | 68 | 109.5 | 27:45 | 47:15 |
| | Paradise Valley Café | 42.4 | 151.9 | 19:10 | 66:25 |
| | San Gorgonio Pass | 57.6 | 209.5 | 30:05 | 96:30 |
| | Van Dusen Canyon | 65.6 | 275.1 | 30:30 | 127:00 |
| 2 | Wrightwood | 88.3 | 363.4 | 40:25 | 167:25 |
| | Acton | 80.8 | 444.2 | 34:00 | 201:25 |
| | Hikertown | 73.4 | 517.6 | 33:50 | 235:15 |
| 3 | Tehachapi (Willow Spr Rd) | 40.9 | 558.5 | 17:55 | 253:10 |
| | Onyx | 94.7 | 653.2 | 41:40 | 294:50 |
| | Kennedy Meadows (S) | 50.2 | 703.4 | 23:10 | 318:00 |
| | Kearsage Pass | 86.7 | 790.1 | 44:05 | 362:05 |
| 4 | VVR | 85.6 | 875.7 | 47:25 | 409:30 |
| | Tuolumne Meadows | 68 | 943.7 | 29:30 | 439:00 |
| | Sonora Pass (KMN) | 74.4 | 1018.1 | 37:50 | 476:50 |
| 5 | S. Lake Tahoe | 73.1 | 1091.2 | 32:25 | 509:15 |
| | Donner Pass | 63.4 | 1154.6 | 29:35 | 538:50 |
| | Sierra City | 42 | 1196.6 | 17:40 | 556:30 |
| | Quincy | 72.5 | 1269.1 | 31:15 | 587:45 |
| 6 | Chester | 63.2 | 1332.3 | 31:50 | 619:35 |
| | Hat Creek/Old Station | 46 | 1378.3 | 18:15 | 637:50 |
| | Burney | 34 | 1412.3 | 14:50 | 652:40 |
| | Castella | 89.9 | 1502.2 | 39:55 | 692:35 |

| 110 days | | 120 days | | 130 days | | 140 days | |
|---|---|---|---|---|---|---|---|
| day | date | day | date | day | date | day | date |
| 1 | May 16 | 1 | May 13 | 1 | May 10 | 1 | May 7 |
| 3 | May 18 | 3 | May 15 | 3 | May 12 | 3 | May 9 |
| 5 | May 20 | 6 | May 18 | 7 | May 16 | 7 | May 13 |
| 7 | May 22 | 8 | May 20 | 9 | May 18 | 9 | May 15 |
| 10 | May 25 | 11 | May 23 | 12 | May 21 | 12 | May 18 |
| 13 | May 28 | 14 | May 26 | 15 | May 24 | 16 | May 22 |
| 16 | May 31 | 18 | May 30 | 19 | May 28 | 21 | May 27 |
| 20 | Jun 4 | 22 | Jun 3 | 24 | Jun 2 | 26 | Jun 1 |
| 23 | Jun 7 | 25 | Jun 6 | 28 | Jun 6 | 30 | Jun 5 |
| 25 | Jun 9 | 27 | Jun 8 | 30 | Jun 8 | 32 | Jun 7 |
| 29 | Jun 13 | 31 | Jun 12 | 34 | Jun 12 | 37 | Jun 12 |
| 31 | Jun 15 | 34 | Jun 15 | 37 | Jun 15 | 40 | Jun 15 |
| 36 | Jun 20 | 39 | Jun 20 | 42 | Jun 20 | 46 | Jun 21 |
| 40 | Jun 24 | 43 | Jun 24 | 47 | Jun 25 | 51 | Jun 26 |
| 43 | Jun 27 | 47 | Jun 28 | 51 | Jun 29 | 55 | Jun 30 |
| 47 | Jul 1 | 51 | Jul 2 | 55 | Jul 3 | 60 | Jul 5 |
| 50 | Jul 4 | 55 | Jul 6 | 59 | Jul 7 | 64 | Jul 9 |
| 53 | Jul 7 | 58 | Jul 9 | 63 | Jul 11 | 68 | Jul 13 |
| 55 | Jul 9 | 60 | Jul 11 | 65 | Jul 13 | 70 | Jul 15 |
| 57 | Jul 11 | 62 | Jul 13 | 67 | Jul 15 | 73 | Jul 18 |
| 59 | Jul 13 | 64 | Jul 15 | 69 | Jul 17 | 76 | Jul 21 |
| 61 | Jul15 | 66 | Jul 17 | 72 | Jul 20 | 78 | Jul 23 |
| 63 | Jul 17 | 68 | Jul 19 | 74 | Jul 22 | 80 | Jul 25 |
| 66 | Jul 20 | 72 | Jul 23 | 78 | Jul 26 | 84 | Jul 29 |

| Section | Resupply Point | Mile | Mile Cum | hr:min | Hr Cum |
|---|---|---|---|---|---|
| | Etna | 98.5 | 1600.7 | 45:00 | 737:35 |
| 7 | Seiad Valley | 56.2 | 1656.9 | 23:55 | 761:30 |
| | Interstate 5 | 62.8 | 1719.7 | 31:05 | 792:35 |
| | Fish Lake Resort | 54.5 | 1774.2 | 22:25 | 815:00 |
| | Mazama Village | 48.5 | 1822.7 | 21:35 | 836:35 |
| 8 | Shelter Cove | 84.9 | 1907.6 | 34:00 | 870:35 |
| | Elk Lake Resort | 45.9 | 1953.5 | 18:20 | 888:55 |
| | Big Lake YC | 42.6 | 1996.1 | 18:20 | 907:15 |
| | Olallie Lake Resort | 52.1 | 2048.2 | 23:45 | 931:00 |
| 9 | Timberline Lodge | 51.4 | 2099.6 | 21:55 | 952:55 |
| | Cascade Locks | 49.7 | 2149.3 | 21:55 | 974:50 |
| | Trout Lake (road 23) | 82.2 | 2231.5 | 38:10 | 1013:00 |
| 10 | White Pass | 66 | 2297.5 | 31:35 | 1044:35 |
| | Snoqualmie Pass | 98.3 | 2395.8 | 45:25 | 1090:00 |
| | Stevens Pass | 70.9 | 2466.7 | 38:35 | 1128:35 |
| 11 | Stehekin | 107.8 | 2574.5 | 50:10 | 1178:45 |
| | Northern Terminus | 80.7 | 2655.2 | 38:40 | 1217:25 |
| **Daily averages** | | | | **2.18mph** | |

| 110 days | | 120 days | | 130 days | | 140 days | |
|---|---|---|---|---|---|---|---|
| day | date | day | date | day | date | day | date |
| 70 | Jul 24 | 76 | Jul 27 | 83 | Jul 31 | 89 | Aug 3 |
| 72 | Jul 26 | 79 | Jul 30 | 86 | Aug 3 | 92 | Aug 6 |
| 75 | Jul 29 | 82 | Aug 2 | 89 | Aug 6 | 96 | Aug 10 |
| 77 | Jul 31 | 83 | Aug 3 | 91 | Aug 8 | 98 | Aug 12 |
| 79 | Aug 2 | 85 | Aug 5 | 93 | Aug10 | 100 | Aug 14 |
| 81 | Aug 4 | 87 | Aug 7 | 95 | Aug 12 | 103 | Aug 17 |
| 83 | Aug 6 | 89 | Aug 9 | 97 | Aug 14 | 105 | Aug 19 |
| 84 | Aug 7 | 91 | Aug 11 | 99 | Aug 16 | 107 | Aug 21 |
| 86 | Aug 9 | 93 | Aug 13 | 101 | Aug 18 | 110 | Aug 24 |
| 88 | Aug 11 | 95 | Aug 15 | 103 | Aug 20 | 112 | Aug 26 |
| 90 | Aug 13 | 97 | Aug 17 | 105 | Aug 22 | 114 | Aug 28 |
| 93 | Aug 16 | 100 | Aug 20 | 109 | Aug 26 | 118 | Sep 1 |
| 95 | Aug 18 | 103 | Aug 23 | 112 | Aug 29 | 121 | Sep 4 |
| 98 | Aug 21 | 107 | Aug 27 | 116 | Sep 2 | 126 | Sep 9 |
| 102 | Aug 25 | 111 | Aug 31 | 121 | Sep 7 | 131 | Sep 14 |
| 107 | Aug 30 | 117 | Sep 6 | 127 | Sep 13 | 137 | Sep 20 |
| 110 | Sep 2 | 120 | Sep 9 | 130 | Sep 16 | 140 | Sep 23 |
| **11:04hr** | **24.1mi** | **10:09hr** | **22.1mi** | **9:22hr** | **20.4mi** | **8:42hr** | **19mi** |

**Table 2** Schedules for 150-, 160-, 170- and 180-day thru-hikes

| Section | Resupply Point | Mile | Mile Cum | hr:min | Hr Cum |
|---|---|---|---|---|---|
| | Southern Terminus | 0 | 0 | 0 | 0 |
| | Mount Laguna | 41.5 | 41.5 | 19:30 | 19:30 |
| 1 | Warner Springs | 68 | 109.5 | 27:45 | 47:15 |
| | Paradise Valley Café | 42.4 | 151.9 | 19:10 | 66:25 |
| | San Gorgonio Pass | 57.6 | 209.5 | 30:05 | 96:30 |
| | Van Dusen Canyon | 65.6 | 275.1 | 30:30 | 127:00 |
| 2 | Wrightwood | 88.3 | 363.4 | 40:25 | 167:25 |
| | Acton | 80.8 | 444.2 | 34:00 | 201:25 |
| | Hikertown | 73.4 | 517.6 | 33:50 | 235:15 |
| 3 | Tehachapi (Willow Spr Rd) | 40.9 | 558.5 | 17:55 | 253:10 |
| | Onyx | 94.7 | 653.2 | 41:40 | 294:50 |
| | Kennedy Meadows (S) | 50.2 | 703.4 | 23:10 | 318:00 |
| | Kearsage Pass | 86.7 | 790.1 | 44:05 | 362:05 |
| 4 | VVR | 85.6 | 875.7 | 47:25 | 409:30 |
| | Tuolumne Meadows | 68 | 943.7 | 29:30 | 439:00 |
| | Sonora Pass (KMN) | 74.4 | 1018.1 | 37:50 | 476:50 |
| 5 | S. Lake Tahoe | 73.1 | 1091.2 | 32:25 | 509:15 |
| | Donner Pass | 63.4 | 1154.6 | 29:35 | 538:50 |
| | Sierra City | 42 | 1196.6 | 17:40 | 556:30 |
| | Quincy | 72.5 | 1269.1 | 31:15 | 587:45 |
| 6 | Chester | 63.2 | 1332.3 | 31:50 | 619:35 |
| | Hat Creek/Old Station | 46 | 1378.3 | 18:15 | 637:50 |
| | Burney | 34 | 1412.3 | 14:50 | 652:40 |
| | Castella | 89.9 | 1502.2 | 39:55 | 692:35 |

| 150 days | | 160 days | | 170 days | | 180 days | |
|---|---|---|---|---|---|---|---|
| **day** | **date** | **day** | **date** | **day** | **date** | **day** | **date** |
| 1 | May 4 | 1 | May 1 | 1 | Apr 28 | 1 | Apr 25 |
| 3 | May 6 | 3 | May 3 | 3 | Apr 30 | 4 | Apr 28 |
| 7 | May 10 | 7 | May 7 | 7 | May 4 | 8 | May 2 |
| 10 | May 13 | 10 | May 10 | 10 | May 7 | 11 | May 5 |
| 13 | May 16 | 14 | May 14 | 14 | May 11 | 15 | May 9 |
| 17 | May 20 | 18 | May 18 | 19 | May 16 | 20 | May 14 |
| 22 | May 25 | 23 | May 23 | 25 | May 22 | 27 | May 21 |
| 28 | May 31 | 30 | May 30 | 32 | May 29 | 34 | May 28 |
| 32 | Jun 4 | 34 | Jun 3 | 36 | Jun 2 | 38 | Jun 1 |
| 34 | Jun 6 | 36 | Jun 5 | 39 | Jun 5 | 41 | Jun 4 |
| 39 | Jun 11 | 42 | Jun 11 | 45 | Jun 11 | 47 | Jun 10 |
| 43 | Jun 15 | 46 | Jun 15 | 49 | Jun 15 | 52 | Jun 15 |
| 49 | Jun 21 | 53 | Jun 22 | 56 | Jun 22 | 60 | Jun 23 |
| 55 | Jun 27 | 59 | Jun 28 | 63 | Jun 29 | 67 | Jun 30 |
| 59 | Jul 1 | 64 | Jul 3 | 68 | Jul 4 | 73 | Jul 6 |
| 64 | Jul 6 | 69 | Jul 8 | 74 | Jul 10 | 79 | Jul 12 |
| 68 | Jul 10 | 74 | Jul 13 | 79 | Jul 15 | 83 | Jul 16 |
| 72 | Jul 14 | 78 | Jul 17 | 83 | Jul 19 | 88 | Jul 21 |
| 74 | Jul 16 | 80 | Jul 19 | 85 | Jul 21 | 90 | Jul 23 |
| 77 | Jul 19 | 83 | Jul 22 | 89 | Jul 25 | 95 | Jul 28 |
| 81 | Jul 23 | 87 | Jul 26 | 93 | Jul 29 | 99 | Aug 1 |
| 84 | Jul 26 | 90 | Jul 29 | 96 | Aug 1 | 102 | Aug 4 |
| 86 | Jul 28 | 92 | Jul 31 | 98 | Aug 3 | 104 | Aug 6 |
| 90 | Aug 1 | 96 | Aug 4 | 102 | Aug 7 | 108 | Aug 10 |

| Section | Resupply Point | Mile | Mile Cum | hr:min | Hr Cum |
|---|---|---|---|---|---|
| | Etna | 98.5 | 1600.7 | 45:00 | 737:35 |
| 7 | Seiad Valley | 56.2 | 1656.9 | 23:55 | 761:30 |
| | Interstate 5 | 62.8 | 1719.7 | 31:05 | 792:35 |
| | Fish Lake Resort | 54.5 | 1774.2 | 22:25 | 815:00 |
| 8 | Mazama Village | 48.5 | 1822.7 | 21:35 | 836:35 |
| | Shelter Cove | 84.9 | 1907.6 | 34:00 | 870:35 |
| | Elk Lake Resort | 45.9 | 1953.5 | 18:20 | 888:55 |
| | Big Lake YC | 42.6 | 1996.1 | 18:20 | 907:15 |
| 9 | Olallie Lake Resort | 52.1 | 2048.2 | 23:45 | 931:00 |
| | Timberline Lodge | 51.4 | 2099.6 | 21:55 | 952:55 |
| | Cascade Locks | 49.7 | 2149.3 | 21:55 | 974:50 |
| | Trout Lake (road 23) | 82.2 | 2231.5 | 38:10 | 1013:00 |
| 10 | White Pass | 66 | 2297.5 | 31:35 | 1044:35 |
| | Snoqualmie Pass | 98.3 | 2395.8 | 45:25 | 1090:00 |
| | Stevens Pass | 70.9 | 2466.7 | 38:35 | 1128:35 |
| 11 | Stehekin | 107.8 | 2574.5 | 50:10 | 1178:45 |
| | Northern Terminus | 80.7 | 2655.2 | 38:40 | 1217:25 |
| **Daily averages** | | | | **2.18mph** | |

| 150 days | | 160 days | | 170 days | | 180 days | |
|---|---|---|---|---|---|---|---|
| **day** | **date** | **day** | **date** | **day** | **date** | **day** | **date** |
| 96 | Aug 7 | 102 | Aug 10 | 109 | Aug 14 | 115 | Aug 17 |
| 99 | Aug 10 | 105 | Aug 13 | 112 | Aug 17 | 119 | Aug 21 |
| 103 | Aug 14 | 110 | Aug 18 | 117 | Aug 22 | 124 | Aug 26 |
| 105 | Aug 16 | 112 | Aug 20 | 119 | Aug 24 | 126 | Aug 28 |
| 108 | Aug 19 | 115 | Aug 23 | 122 | Aug 27 | 130 | Sep 1 |
| 111 | Aug 22 | 118 | Aug 26 | 125 | Aug 30 | 134 | Sep 5 |
| 113 | Aug 24 | 121 | Aug 29 | 129 | Sep 3 | 137 | Sep 8 |
| 115 | Aug 26 | 123 | Aug 31 | 131 | Sep 5 | 139 | Sep 10 |
| 118 | Aug 29 | 126 | Sep 3 | 134 | Sep 8 | 142 | Sep 13 |
| 120 | Aug 31 | 129 | Sep 6 | 137 | Sep 11 | 145 | Sep 16 |
| 122 | Sep 2 | 131 | Sep 8 | 140 | Sep14 | 148 | Sep 19 |
| 126 | Sep 6 | 135 | Sep 12 | 144 | Sep 18 | 153 | Sep 24 |
| 130 | Sep 10 | 139 | Sep 16 | 148 | Sep 22 | 157 | Sep 28 |
| 135 | Sep 15 | 144 | Sep 21 | 153 | Sep 27 | 163 | Oct 4 |
| 140 | Sep 20 | 149 | Sep 26 | 159 | Oct 3 | 169 | Oct 10 |
| 146 | Sep 26 | 156 | Oct 3 | 166 | Oct 10 | 176 | Oct 17 |
| 150 | Sep 30 | 160 | Oct 7 | 170 | Oct 14 | 180 | Oct 21 |
| **8:07hr** | **17.7mi** | **7:36hr** | **16.6mi** | **7:10hr** | **15.6mi** | **6:46hr** | **14.75mi** |

*The trail in Washington often traverses steep slopes that would become dangerous in snow (Stage 94)*

# APPENDIX E

## *Detailed schedule for an easy-going start*

*First view of Mount Shasta at sunset (Stage 56)*

If you feel like you might prefer to start a little earlier and build up quite gradually over the first few weeks, then the table below is for you. The timings are based on walking at a leisurely 2mph, with longer and shorter days alternating initially to build up fitness. Across these first (almost) four weeks, the average daily distance is 11 miles, which equates to an average of 5hr 30min of daily walking.

Taking things gently to start with will protect your joints, minimize any trouble from blisters, give you more time to experiment with tent pitches and packing, and generally get into the rhythm of daily hiking. Getting trail-fit more gradually will reduce some of the soreness as your body hardens up to carrying a pack too.

The earlier start should also increase the likelihood of more water sources being available for you in the early desert stages. Some sources will dry out quite quickly across late April to early May.

This schedule adds seven days to the 180-day schedule by starting on April 18. If you then pick up the 180-day schedule from Big Bear City on May 14, you will get to Kennedy Meadows by June 15.

You might find that further along the trail you are traveling a little faster/further each day and 'catch up' with the 170-day or even the 160-day schedule.

In addition to the detailed timings and suggested overnight tent site locations, I have added detailed resupply notes to the schedule. This should help you to get used to thinking ahead and planning resupply options, as well as prevent you carrying too much out of Campo on day one – a common mistake. There are plenty of resupply options in these early stages and no need to carry a heavy food bag while you are getting used to carrying a pack.

**Table 3** Detailed schedule for an easy-going start

| Day | Camp | Mile point | Daily miles | Daily hours |
|---|---|---|---|---|
| 1 | Hauser Mountain | 9 | 9 | 4.5 |
| 2 | Lake Morena Campground | 20 | 11 | 5.5 |
| 3 | Boulder Oaks Campground | 26 | 6 | 3 |
| 4 | Long Canyon Creek | 37 | 11 | 5.5 |
| 5 | Mount Laguna | 42 | 5 | 2.5 |
| 6 | Pioneer Mail Trailhead | 53 | 11 | 5.5 |
| 7 | Rodriguez Spur Truck Trail | 68 | 15 | 7.5 |
| 8 | San Felipe Creek/Scissors Crossing | 77 | 9 | 4.5 |
| 9 | San Felipe Hills/3rd gate water cache | 91 | 14 | 7 |
| 10 | Barrel Spring | 101 | 10 | 5 |
| 11 | Warner Springs | 110 | 9 | 4.5 |
| 12 | Lost Valley Road (near Spring) | 120 | 10 | 5 |
| 13 | Tule Canyon Road | 137 | 17 | 8.5 |
| 14 | Highway 74 | 152 | 15 | 7.5 |
| 15 | Cedar Spring | 163 | 11 | 5.5 |
| 16 | Apache Spring | 169 | 6 | 3 |

| Stage | Date | Resupply |
|---|---|---|
| 1 | April 18 | Leave Campo with food for days 1 and 2 plus an extra couple of main meals |
| 1 | April 19 | Eat at Oak Shores Malt Shop and supplement carried food for days 3–5 |
| 2 | April 20 | |
| 2 | April 21 | |
| 2 | April 22 | Eat at restaurant and collect parcel sent in advance, food for days 6–8 |
| 3 | April 23 | |
| 3 | April 24 | |
| 3 | April 25 | Hitch to Julian, eat there, and return with food for days 9–11 |
| 4 | April 26 | |
| 4 | April 27 | Could also get a ride out to Ranchita store, shower, eat and return, picking up food for days 11–14, or use day 11 option: |
| 4 | April 28 | Pick up a package from PO, sent in advance for days 12-14 |
| 5 | April 29 | |
| 6 | April 30 | |
| 6 | May 1 | Walk/hitch 1 mile to Paradise Valley Café, eat and collect package: food for days 15–17 |
| 7 | May 2 | |
| 7 | May 3 | |

| Day | Camp | Mile point | Daily miles | Daily hours | |
|---|---|---|---|---|---|
| 17 | Idyllwild (from Saddle Junction) | 179 | 10 | 5 | |
| 18 | Fuller Ridge Campground | 191 | 12 | 6 | |
| 19 | Snow Canyon | 206 | 15 | 7.5 | |
| 20 | Tamarack Rd (for Cabazon) | 210 | 4 | 2 | |
| 21 | Whitewater River Preserve | 219 | 9 | 4.5 | |
| 22 | Fork Springs | 232 | 13 | 6.5 | |
| 23 | Coon Creek Cabin | 246 | 14 | 7 | |
| 24 | Arrastre Trail Camp | 256 | 10 | 5 | |
| 25 | Van Dusen Canyon | 275 | 19 | 9.5 | |
| 26 | Walk 4 miles to Big Bear City, zero-day, resupply, return to camp at Van Dusen Canyon | | | | |
| 27 | Depart on 180-day schedule | | | | |
| **Daily averages** | | | **11mi** | **5.5hrs** | |

| Stage | Date | Resupply |
|---|---|---|
| 7 | May 4 | Walk 2.5 miles to trailhead then hitch to Idyllwild, use state park campground, laundry, resupply for days 18–20 |
| 8 | May 5 | Walk/hitch to trail early AM |
| 8 | May 6 | |
| 8 | May 7 | Hitch to Cabazon PO to collect pre-sent package, or Banning for supermarkets; resupply for days 21–25 |
| 9 | May 8 | |
| 9 | May 9 | |
| 9 | May 10 | |
| 10 | May 11 | |
| 10 | May 12 | Take a zero tomorrow, do laundry, eat, resupply and depart on May 14 on 180-day schedule |
| | May 13 | |
| | May 14 | |

*Color lines the trail below volcanic outcrops in Mokelumne Wilderness (Stage 39)*

## DOWNLOAD THE GPX FILES

All the routes in this guide are available for download from:

**www.cicerone.co.uk/1212/GPX**

as standard format GPX files. You should be able to load them into most online GPX systems and mobile devices, whether GPS or smartphone. You may need to convert the file into your preferred format using a conversion programme such as gpsvisualizer.com or one of the many other such websites and programmes.

When you follow this link, you will be asked for your email address and where you purchased the guidebook, and have the option to subscribe to the Cicerone e-newsletter.

www.cicerone.co.uk

# LISTING OF CICERONE GUIDES

### BRITISH ISLES CHALLENGES, COLLECTIONS AND ACTIVITIES

Great Walks on the England Coast Path
Map and Compass
The Big Rounds
The Book of the Bivvy
The Book of the Bothy
The Mountains of England and Wales:
Vol 1 Wales
Vol 2 England
The National Trails
Walking the End to End Trail

### SHORT WALKS SERIES

Short Walks Hadrian's Wall
Short Walks Lake District — Keswick, Borrowdale and Buttermere
Short Walks Lake District — Windermere Ambleside and Grasmere
Short Walks Lake District — Coniston and Langdale
Short Walks in Arnside and Silverdale
Short Walks in Nidderdale
Short Walks in Northumberland: Wooler, Rothbury, Alnwick and the coast
Short Walks on the Malvern Hills
Short Walks in Cornwall: Falmouth and the Lizard
Short Walks in Cornwall: Land's End and Penzance
Short Walks in the South Downs: Brighton, Eastbourne and Arundel
Short Walks in the Surrey Hills
Short Walks on Dartmoor — South: Ivybridge and Princetown
Short Walks on Exmoor
Short Walks Winchester
Short Walks in Pembrokeshire: Tenby and the south
Short Walks in Dumfries and Galloway
Short Walks on the Isle of Mull
Short Walks on the Orkney Islands
Short Walks on the Shetland Islands

### SCOTLAND

Ben Nevis and Glen Coe
Cycling in the Hebrides
Cycling the North Coast 500
Great Mountain Days in Scotland
Mountain Biking in Southern and Central Scotland
Mountain Biking in West and North West Scotland
Not the West Highland Way
Scotland
Scotland's Best Small Mountains
Scotland's Mountain Ridges
Scottish Wild Country Backpacking
Skye's Cuillin Ridge Traverse
The Borders Abbeys Way
The Great Glen Way
The Great Glen Way Map Booklet
The Hebridean Way
The Hebrides
The Isle of Mull
The Isle of Skye
The Skye Trail
The Southern Upland Way
The West Highland Way
Walking Ben Lawers, Rannoch and Atholl
Walking in the Cairngorms
Walking in the Pentland Hills
Walking in the Scottish Borders
Walking in the Southern Uplands
Walking in Torridon, Fisherfield, Fannichs and An Teallach
Walking Loch Lomond and the Trossachs
Walking on Arran
Walking on Harris and Lewis
Walking on Jura, Islay and Colonsay
Walking on Rum and the Small Isles
Walking on the Orkney and Shetland Isles
Walking on Uist and Barra
Walking the Cape Wrath Trail
Walking the Corbetts Vol 1 South of the Great Glen
Walking the Corbetts Vol 2 North of the Great Glen
Walking the Fife Pilgrim Way
Walking the Galloway Hills
Walking the John o' Groats Trail
Walking the Munros
Vol 1 — Southern, Central and Western Highlands
Vol 2 — Northern Highlands and the Cairngorms
Walking the West Highland Way
West Highland Way Map Booklet
Winter Climbs in the Cairngorms
Winter Climbs: Ben Nevis and Glen Coe

### NORTHERN ENGLAND ROUTES

Cycling the Reivers Route
Cycling the Way of the Roses
Hadrian's Cycleway
Hadrian's Wall Path
Hadrian's Wall Path Map Booklet
The Coast to Coast Cycle Route
The Coast to Coast Map Booklet
The Coast to Coast Walk
The Pennine Way
Pennine Way Map Booklet
Walking the Dales Way
The Dales Way Map Booklet

### LAKE DISTRICT

Bikepacking in the Lake District
Cycling in the Lake District
Great Mountain Days in the Lake District
Joss Naylor's Lakes, Meres and Waters of the Lake District
Lake District Winter Climbs
Lake District: High Level and Fell Walks
Lake District: Low Level and Lake Walks
Mountain Biking in the Lake District
Outdoor Adventures with Children — Lake District
Scrambles in the Lake District —
North
South
Trail and Fell Running in the Lake District
Walking The Cumbria Way
Walking the Lake District Fells —
Borrowdale
Buttermere
Coniston
Keswick
Langdale
Mardale and the Far East
Patterdale
Wasdale
Walking the Tour of the Lake District

### NORTH-WEST ENGLAND AND THE ISLE OF MAN

Cycling the Pennine Bridleway
Isle of Man Coastal Path
The Lancashire Cycleway
The Lune Valley and Howgills
Walking in Cumbria's Eden Valley
Walking in Lancashire
Walking in the Forest of Bowland and Pendle
Walking on the Isle of Man
Walking on the West Pennine Moors
Walking the Ribble Way
Walks in Silverdale and Arnside

### NORTH-EAST ENGLAND, YORKSHIRE DALES AND PENNINES

Cycling in the Yorkshire Dales
Great Mountain Days in the Pennines
Mountain Biking in the Yorkshire Dales
The Cleveland Way and the Yorkshire Wolds Way
The Cleveland Way Map Booklet
The North York Moors
Trail and Fell Running in the Yorkshire Dales
Walking in County Durham

Walking in Northumberland
Walking in the North Pennines
Walking in the Yorkshire Dales:
North and East
South and West
Walking St Cuthbert's Way
Walking St Oswald's Way and Northumberland Coast Path

**DERBYSHIRE, PEAK DISTRICT AND MIDLANDS**

Cycling in the Peak District
Dark Peak Walks
Scrambles in the Dark Peak
Walking in Derbyshire
Walking in the Peak District —
White Peak East
White Peak West

**WALES AND WELSH BORDERS**

Cycle Touring in Wales
Cycling Lon Las Cymru
Great Mountain Days in Snowdonia
Hillwalking in Shropshire
Mountain Walking in Snowdonia
Offa's Dyke Path
Offa's Dyke Map Booklet
The Pembrokeshire Coast Path
Pembrokeshire Coast Path Map Booklet
Scrambles in Snowdonia
Snowdonia: 30 Low-level and Easy Walks — North, South
The Cambrian Way
The Snowdonia Way
The Wye Valley Walk
Walking Glyndwr's Way
Walking in Carmarthenshire
Walking in Pembrokeshire
Walking in the Brecon Beacons
Walking in the Wye Valley
Walking on Gower
Walking the Severn Way
Walking the Shropshire Way
Walking the Wales Coast Path

**SOUTHERN ENGLAND**

20 Classic Sportive Rides in South East England
20 Classic Sportive Rides in South West England
Cycling in the Cotswolds
Mountain Biking on the North Downs
Mountain Biking on the South Downs
The North Downs Way
North Downs Way Map Booklet
Walking the South West Coast Path
South West Coast Path Map Booklet
— Vol 1: Minehead to St Ives
— Vol 2: St Ives to Plymouth
— Vol 3: Plymouth to Poole
Suffolk Coast and Heath Walks
The Cotswold Way
The Cotswold Way Map Booklet
The Kennet and Avon Canal
The Lea Valley Walk
The Peddars Way and Norfolk Coast Path
The Pilgrims' Way
The Ridgeway National Trail
The Ridgeway Map Booklet
The South Downs Way
The South Downs Way Map Booklet
The Thames Path
The Thames Path Map Booklet
The Two Moors Way
Two Moors Way Map Booklet
Walking Hampshire's Test Way
Walking in Cornwall
Walking in Essex
Walking in Kent
Walking in London
Walking in Norfolk
Walking in the Chilterns
Walking in the Cotswolds
Walking in the Isles of Scilly
Walking in the New Forest
Walking in the North Wessex Downs
Walking on Dartmoor
Walking on Guernsey
Walking on Jersey
Walking on the Isle of Wight
Walking the Dartmoor Way
Walking the Jurassic Coast
Walking the Sarsen Way
Walks in the South Downs National Park
Cycling Land's End to John o' Groats

**ALPS CROSS-BORDER ROUTES**

100 Hut Walks in the Alps
Alpine Ski Mountaineering Vol 1 — Western Alps
The Karnischer Hohenweg
The Tour of the Bernina
Trekking the Tour du Mont Blanc
Tour du Mont Blanc Map Booklet
Trail Running — Chamonix and the Mont Blanc region
Trekking Chamonix to Zermatt
Trekking in the Alps
Trekking in the Silvretta and Ratikon Alps
Trekking Munich to Venice
Walking in the Alps

**FRANCE, BELGIUM, AND LUXEMBOURG**

Camino de Santiago — Via Podiensis
Chamonix Mountain Adventures
Cycling London to Paris
Cycling the Canal de la Garonne
Cycling the Canal du Midi
Mont Blanc Walks
Mountain Adventures in the Maurienne
Short Treks on Corsica
The Grand Traverse of the Massif Central
The Moselle Cycle Route
Trekking in the Vanoise
Trekking the Cathar Way
Trekking the GR10
Trekking the GR20 Corsica
Trekking the Robert Louis Stevenson Trail
The GR5 Trail
The GR5 Trail —
Vosges and Jura
Benelux and Lorraine
Via Ferratas of the French Alps
Walking in Provence — East
Walking in Provence — West
Walking in the Auvergne
Walking in the Brianconnais
Walking in the Dordogne
Walking in the Haute Savoie: North
Walking in the Haute Savoie: South
Walking on Corsica
Walking the Brittany Coast Path
Walking in the Ardennes

**PYRENEES AND FRANCE/SPAIN CROSS-BORDER ROUTES**

Shorter Treks in the Pyrenees
The Pyrenean Haute Route
The Pyrenees
Trekking the Cami dels Bons Homes
Trekking the GR11 Trail
Walks and Climbs in the Pyrenees

**SPAIN AND PORTUGAL**

Camino de Santiago: Camino Frances
Costa Blanca Mountain Adventures
Cycling the Camino de Santiago
Mountain Walking in Mallorca
Mountain Walking in Southern Catalunya
Spain's Sendero Historico: The GR1
The Andalucian Coast to Coast Walk
The Camino del Norte and Camino Primitivo
The Camino Ingles and Ruta do Mar
The Mountains Around Nerja
The Mountains of Ronda and Grazalema
The Sierras of Extremadura
Trekking in Mallorca
Trekking in the Canary Islands
Trekking the GR7 in Andalucia
Walking and Trekking in the Sierra Nevada
Walking in Andalucia
Walking in Catalunya —
Barcelona
Girona Pyrenees
Walking in the Picos de Europa
Walking La Via de la Plata and Camino Sanabres
Walking on Gran Canaria
Walking on La Gomera and El Hierro
Walking on La Palma
Walking on Lanzarote and Fuerteventura
Walking on Tenerife
Walking on the Costa Blanca
Walking the Camino dos Faros
Portugal's Rota Vicentina

The Camino Portugues
Walking in Portugal
Walking in the Algarve
Walking on Madeira
Walking on the Azores

**SWITZERLAND**
Switzerland's Jura Crest Trail
The Swiss Alps
Tour of the Jungfrau Region
Trekking the Swiss Via Alpina
Walking in Arolla and Zinal
Walking in the Bernese Oberland — Jungfrau region
Walking in the Engadine — Switzerland
Walking in the Valais
Walking in Ticino
Walking in Zermatt and Saas-Fee

**GERMANY**
Hiking and Cycling in the Black Forest
The Danube Cycleway Vol 1
The Rhine Cycle Route
The Westweg
Walking in the Bavarian Alps

**POLAND, SLOVAKIA, ROMANIA, HUNGARY AND BULGARIA**
The Danube Cycleway Vol 2
The High Tatras
The Mountains of Romania

**SCANDINAVIA, ICELAND AND GREENLAND**
Hiking in Norway — North
Hiking in Norway — South
Trekking the Kungsleden
Trekking in Greenland — The Arctic Circle Trail
Walking and Trekking in Iceland

**SLOVENIA, CROATIA, SERBIA, MONTENEGRO AND ALBANIA**
Hiking Slovenia's Juliana Trail
Mountain Biking in Slovenia
The Islands of Croatia
The Julian Alps of Slovenia
The Mountains of Montenegro
The Peaks of the Balkans Trail
The Slovene Mountain Trail
Walking in Slovenia: The Karavanke
Walks and Treks in Croatia

**ITALY**
Alta Via 1 — Trekking in the Dolomites
Alta Via 2 — Trekking in the Dolomites
Day Walks in the Dolomites
Italy's Grande Traversata delle Alpi
Italy's Sibillini National Park
Ski Touring and Snowshoeing in the Dolomites
The Way of St Francis
Trekking Gran Paradiso: Alta Via 2
Trekking in the Apennines
Trekking the Giants' Trail: Alta Via 1 through the Italian Pennine Alps
Via Ferratas of the Italian Dolomites:
Vol 1
Vol 2
Walking in Abruzzo
Walking in Italy's Cinque Terre
Walking in Italy's Stelvio National Park
Walking in Sicily
Walking in the Aosta Valley
Walking in the Dolomites
Walking in Tuscany
Walking in Umbria
Walking Lake Como and Maggiore
Walking Lake Garda and Iseo
Walking on the Amalfi Coast
Walking the Via Francigena Pilgrim Route — Part 2
Walking the Via Francigena Pilgrim Route — Part 3
Walks and Treks in the Maritime Alps

**IRELAND**
The Wild Atlantic Way and Western Ireland
Walking the Kerry Way
Walking the Wicklow Way

**EUROPEAN CYCLING**
Cycling the Route des Grandes Alpes
Cycling the Ruta Via de la Plata
The Elbe Cycle Route
The River Loire Cycle Route
The River Rhone Cycle Route

**INTERNATIONAL CHALLENGES, COLLECTIONS AND ACTIVITIES**
Europe's High Points
Walking the Via Francigena Pilgrim Route — Part 1

**AUSTRIA**
Innsbruck Mountain Adventures
Trekking Austria's Adlerweg
Trekking in Austria's Hohe Tauern
Trekking in Austria's Stubai Alps
Trekking in Austria's Zillertal Alps
Walking in Austria
Walking in the Salzkammergut: the Austrian Lake District

**MEDITERRANEAN**
The High Mountains of Crete
Trekking in Greece
Walking and Trekking in Zagori
Walking and Trekking on Corfu
Walking on the Greek Islands — the Cyclades
Walking in Cyprus
Walking on Malta

**HIMALAYA**
8000 metres
Everest: A Trekker's Guide
Trekking in the Karakoram

**NORTH AMERICA**
Hiking and Cycling the California Missions Trail
The John Muir Trail
The Pacific Crest Trail

**SOUTH AMERICA**
Aconcagua and the Southern Andes
Hiking and Biking Peru's Inca Trails
Trekking in Torres del Paine

**AFRICA**
Kilimanjaro
Walking in the Drakensberg
Walks and Scrambles in the Moroccan Anti-Atlas

**NEW ZEALAND AND AUSTRALIA**
Hiking the Overland Track

**CHINA, JAPAN, AND ASIA**
Annapurna
Hiking and Trekking in the Japan Alps and Mount Fuji
Hiking in Hong Kong
Japan's Kumano Kodo Pilgrimage
Japan's Kumano Kodo Pilgrimage
Trekking in Bhutan
Trekking in Ladakh
Trekking in Tajikistan
Trekking in the Himalaya

**TECHNIQUES**
Fastpacking
The Mountain Hut Book

**MINI GUIDES**
Alpine Flowers
Navigation
Pocket First Aid and Wilderness Medicine

**MOUNTAIN LITERATURE**
A Walk in the Clouds
Abode of the Gods
Fifty Years of Adventure
The Pennine Way — the Path, the People, the Journey
Unjustifiable Risk?

For full information on all our guides, books and eBooks, visit our website:
**www.cicerone.co.uk**